Better Homes and Gardens®

FURNITURE PROJECTS
YOU CAN BUILD

BETTER HOMES AND GARDENS® BOOKS

Editorial Director: Don Dooley
Executive Editor: Gerald M. Knox
Art Director: Ernest Shelton Asst. Art Director: Randal Yontz
Production and Copy Editor: David Kirchner
Building and Remodeling Editor: Noel Seney
Building Books Editor: Larry Clayton
Contributing Architectural Editor: Stephen Mead
Remodeling and Home Maintenance Editor: David R. Haupert
Building Ideas Editor: Douglas M. Lidster
Remodeling Ideas Editor: Dan Kaercher
Kitchens, Appliances, Home Management Editor: Joan McCloskey
Associate Editors: Kristelle Petersen, Cheryl Scott
Graphic Designers: Harijs Priekulis, Faith Berven,
Sheryl Veenschoten, Rich Lewis

CONTENTS

SENSATIONAL SEATING 4

TERRIFIC TABLES 14

ARTFUL ACTIVITY CENTERS 24

FURNITURE BY THE ROOMFUL 34

BEDS AND BOARDS 48

SENSIBLE STORAGE 58

FOR CHILDREN ONLY 68

OUTDOOR PROJECTS 76

THE AMAZING CUBE 84

FURNITURE BUILDING BASICS 85

COMMON MATERIALS—85
WOOD JOINERY TECHNIQUES—86
THE HARDWARE YOU'LL NEED—90
HOW TO MAKE DRAWERS—92

HOW TO INSTALL CABINET DOORS—93
FINISHING TECHNIQUES—94
HOW TO UPHOLSTER CUSHIONS—95
COMMON FURNITURE DIMENSIONS—96

SENSA-TIONAL SEATING

Looking for a seating unit that's more than just a place to relax—something that will add some pizzazz to your decor? If so, you'll appreciate the projects presented here. Each is as much a conversation piece as it is a center of conversation.

And what's more, you don't have to sacrifice comfort for good looks. From the dramatic swinging sofa pictured here to the move-anywhere modular grouping, each project is designed with your comfort in mind.

A seating unit is only as comfortable as its cushions, however, so be sure to read page 95 for tips on making the cushions for your project. You'll find that making professional-looking cushions isn't that big a hassle after all.

Why settle for uninteresting, uninspiring seating? Just look through these thought-provoking projects and you'll see there's really no need to.

SWINGING SOFA

For sheer visual impact, few projects can rival this sofa. And its floating-on-air comfort makes it as functional as it is striking. A popular choice for family and rec rooms, it's surprisingly easy to make from a solid-core door and some chain.

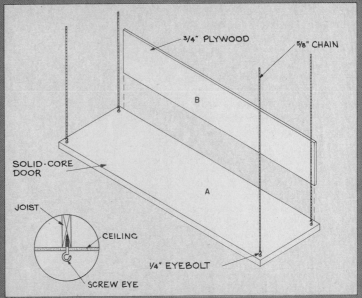

1 Locate ceiling joists with a stud finder or drive small nails into ceiling. Most ceiling joists are 16 inches on center.
2 Mark the joists for eyebolts in a rectangular formation as close to the size of the seat as possible. If you cannot place swing seat directly under the eyebolts, chains will have a slightly splayed appearance, but this will not interfere with the swing's movement. If you can place the swing at right angles to the joists, chains will hang closer to perpendicular.
3 Drill joists for screw eyes.
4 Attach eyes to joists (see detail), and hang lengths of chain (lengths will vary with ceiling heights) so that swing seat is 16 to 18 inches from the floor.
5 Drill holes in solid-core door

(A) 1 inch in from ends and sides; secure eyebolts.
6 Center, glue, and screw plywood back (B) to seat with 3-inch wood screws centered every 6 inches.
7 Upholster mattress and bolster (see page 95).
8 Secure unit to chains at eyebolts. (For greater stability, secure back to chains with screw eyes, and add arm rests.)
9 Paint or stain sofa.

Materials (for project shown):
³/₄-in. plywood—¹/₂ sht.

  B 1 18×76 in.
30×80-in. solid core door (A), lengths of ⁵/₈-in. chain, foam cushion for seat, tapered bolster for back, fabric to cover both, ¹/₄-in. eyebolts, screw eyes, and stain or paint.

SUPER-CHIC SEATING

Double thicknesses of mitered 2x6s provide sturdy support for this low-back chair. In fact, the construction is so solid that you can extend all horizontal pieces to make the matching sofa shown in the background. Versatile, sturdy, attractive seating—what else could you ask for?

1 Miter 2x6 chair arm pieces (A, B) at 45 degrees. Glue and nail double thicknesses together, and assemble sides. (For an extra-sturdy mitered joint, use dowels—refer to page 88.)

2 Glue and nail seat frame sides (C) to legs so that top of 2x6 seat frame piece measures 12 inches from the floor (foam cushion will add more height).

3 Bevel exposed vertical edge of backs (D) and seat frame front (E) pieces. Glue and nail backs to legs, and seat frame front to seat frame sides.

4 Glue and nail 1x2 ledgers (F, G) to inside of seat frame, recessed ¾ inch for plywood.

5 Secure plywood seat (H).

6 Upholster cushions (see page 95) with desired fabric.

7 Sand unit; finish as desired.

Materials (for chair shown):

2×6—44 ft.
A,C	6 27 in.	**B**	8 25 in.
D	2 30 in.	**E**	1 24 in.

1×2—8 ft.
F	2 25½ in.	**G**	2 21 in.

¾-in. plywood—¼ sht.
H	1 21×27 in.

Glue, paint or stain and varnish, foam cushions, upholstery fabric.

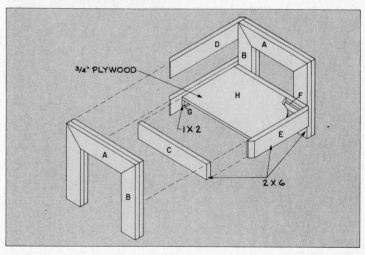

ROUGH 'N READY CANVAS CHAIR

Old-fashioned canvas sling chairs were never this comfortable—or this easy to make. Rope secured in a sturdy frame supports the natural canvas seat. If you're a purist, feel free to use striped circus-tent fabric instead.

1 Round off tops of uprights (A, B). Drill ½-inch holes at center of arc in the top of each upright. Cut a ½-inch-deep dado at bottom of uprights for lower bracing (refer to page 87 for tips on making this joint).

2 Construct lower bracing assembly of 5/4x3 pieces (C, D). Glue and screw together. Butt-join bracing to uprights at dadoes.

3 Glue and screw back brace (E) between uprights as shown.

4 Cut lengths of 1½-inch plastic pipe for guards to support rope and canvas sling

5 Sand; finish chair.

6 Position plastic guards between uprights at top and bottom. Thread ¾-inch rope through holes and guards. Pull taut (but not tight); secure by knotting as shown in detail.

7 Make canvas sling from four pieces of fabric to obtain shaping. Two sidepieces are triangular, and the "seat" and "back" are trapezoid shapes. (Use an old bed sheet or other fabric to make a pattern before cutting canvas, and adjust shaping, if necessary.) Add contrasting top-stitching if desired.

8 Position sling on chair, turn ends under, and hand-stitch.

Materials (for project shown):

5/4×3—18 ft.

A,D	4	18 in.	**B**	2	30 in.
C	2	24 in.	**E**	1	19¼ in.

Approximately 1 yd. 42-in.-wide fabric, length of ¾-in. rope, 1½-in. plastic pipe or old garden hose, glue, stain, and varnish.

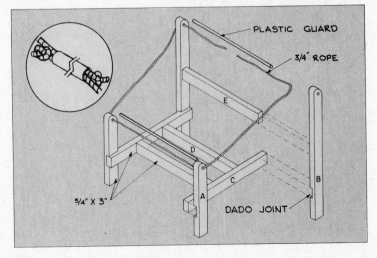

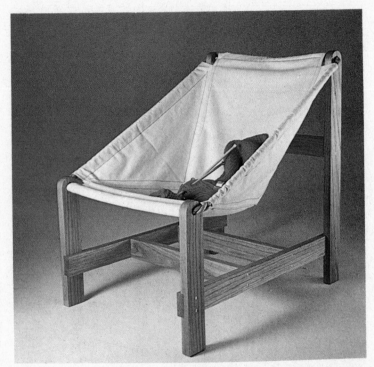

PLASTIC GUARD

3/4" ROPE

E

D

C

A

B

5/4" X 3"

DADO JOINT

HIGH-STYLE PLATFORM SEATING

If a hard-to-decorate corner has you stumped, this unit may be just what you need. A cozy seating nook carved out of a plywood platform makes a great place for conversation or listening to music. And you can carpet the upper deck to match your room decor.

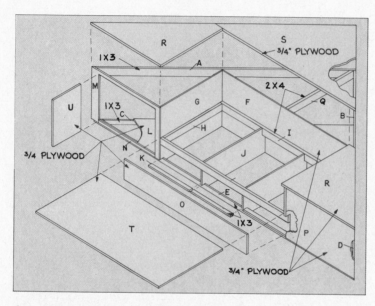

1 Angle-cut and bolt 1x3 nailers (A, B, C, D) to wall. Angle-cut and nail 1x3 (E) to frame.

2 Build inner box of three plywood pieces (F, G), notching side pieces (G) for toe space.

3 Glue and screw 2x4 seat supports (H, I) to inside of box. Be sure to notch the plywood supports (J), and then toenail them to the floor.

4 Glue and nail 1x3 filler strips (K) to unit as shown. Secure floor (L) to inside.

5 Glue and nail facing pieces (M, N, O, P) to unit (making rectangular cutout in door front).

6 Glue and nail angle-cut joist (Q) to top at center corner.

7 Nail pieces R, S, and T to frame.

8 Hang doors (U).

9 Sand; paint or stain.

Materials (for project shown):

3/4-in. plywood—6 shts.

T	1	39×75 in.
F	1	28×76½ in.
J	2	13×38¼ in.
O	1	10½×75 in.
U	2	18×22 in.
G	2	28×38¼ in.
M,P	2	25½×42 in.
L	1	41¼×41¼×58⅜ in.
S	1	57¼×57¼×81 in.
R	2	42×42×59⅜ in.

1×3—42 ft.

A	1	9 ft. 3½ in.			
B	1	9 ft. 2 in.			
C	1	54 in.	D	1	37 in.
E	1	12 ft. 10⅞ in.			
K	3	24½ in.			

2×4—26 ft.

I	2	75 in.	Q	1	39¾ in.
H	2	35¼ in.			

1×2—3 ft.

N	1	36 in.

Glue, hinges, and paint or stain.

MOVE-AROUND MODULAR SEATING

If you're a person who enjoys changing the look of your rooms from time to time, you'll love this seating idea. You can mix-and-match to your heart's content and produce an entirely different look every time. The photos at left show several of the exciting possibilities.

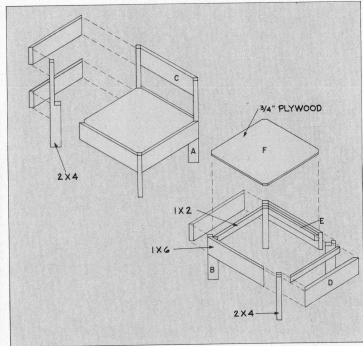

1 From taller uprights (A), cut a 14½-inch-long notch so that remainder of 2x4 measures 1½ inches wide. From shorter 2x4 uprights (B), cut a ½-inch-long notch the same width.

2 Cut a 45-degree miter from pieces C, D, and E as shown.

3 Glue and nail mitered surround pieces to uprights. Glue and nail recessed ledger strips to inside of seat frame.

4 Cut four corners from ½-inch plywood base (F) so that cut edge measures 1½ inches. Glue and nail to ledgers. For table, apply plastic laminate to plywood top.

5 Wrap cushions with batting and upholster (see page 95).

6 Sand; finish.

Materials (for each module):

2×4—6 to 10 ft.

For table or ottoman—6 ft.
B	4	14 in.			

For chair—8 ft.
A	2	28 in.	**B**	2	14 in.

For corner unit—10 ft.
A	3	28 in.	**B**	1	14 in.

1×2—8 ft.
E	4	27⅞ in.			

1×6—8 to 12 ft.
D	4	29½ in.	**C**	1 or 2	29½ in.

½-in. plywood—½ sht.
F	1	30×30 in.			

Foam cushions, batting, fabric, glue, stain, and varnish.

TWO-SEATER SOFA

In terms of comfort, looks, and function, this no-frills, clean-lined sofa compares favorably with any of its store-bought counterparts. But there *is* one big difference you'll notice right away—the cost. Built of fir, plywood, and 2-inch framing, this unit is much easier on your pocketbook.

1 Assemble 2x4s (A, B) as shown in sketch. Glue and nail 2x2 seat frame (C, D) together.
2 Attach casters to 2x4 frame.
3 Position together 2x10s (E) for sides. Glue and nail to bottom frame and seat frame assemblies. Keep front edges of frames flush with each other and recessed from front edge of 2x10s for 1x10 and 1x4 trim. Also allow a ½-inch space between bottom of caster and 2x10s.
4 Glue and screw back (F) between sides.
5 Miter 2x3 cap pieces (G, H); glue and nail in place.
6 Glue and nail plywood seat (N) to 2x2 frame.
7 Glue and nail 1x12 (I) to front (see sketch).
8 Miter inside and outside corners of 1x4 trim (J, K, L, M). Glue and nail in place.
9 Sand unit; finish as desired.
10 Wrap foam cushions with batting; upholster (see page 95).

Materials (for project shown):

³/₄-in. plywood—2 shts.

F	1	28×57 in.	**N** 1 24¾×57 in.

2×10—14 ft.

E	6	28 in.

2×4—14 ft.

A	2	54 in.	**B**	2 23¾ in.

2×3—12 ft.

G	2	30 in.	**H**	1 62 in.

2×2—14 ft.

C	2	54 in.	**D**	2 24¾ in.

1×12—6 ft.

I	1	57 in.

1×4—12 ft.

J	2	29¼ in.	**K**	1 57 in.
L	2	2¼ in.	**M**	2 3 in.

Four casters, glue, paint or stain, batting, foam cushions, and fabric.

REC ROOM/DEN LOUNGE DUO

No matter where you put these ruggedly attractive lounges, it's a good bet they'll get plenty of use. And rightly so! They're great for a host of leisure-time activities—reading, watching TV, and, of course, snoozing.

1 Miter ends of 2x6 frame pieces (A, B). Glue and nail together.
2 To notch uprights (C, D) for bed frame, mark each post for a notch to accept a 2x6. (Top of notch should be 18 inches from the floor.) Start saw cut on these marks and continue sawing until cut edge measures 2¼ inches. Chisel out rounded edge of post. Chisel inward at right angles along the edge of this vertical plane until you have cut a 1½x1½-inch wedge (see detail).
3 Toenail bed frame to posts from inside.
4 Miter, glue, and nail 1x2 ledgers (E, F) to inside of bed frame.
5 Notch 2x4 supports (G) around ledgers. Space equally along frame; glue and nail in place.
6 Glue and nail plywood (H) to ledgers and supports.
7 Chisel off a flat area on taller uprights, and toenail headboard (I) between them.
8 Sand; finish as desired.
9 Add upholstered mattress (see page 95).

Materials (for each lounge):

¾-in. plywood—1 sht.
  H 1 39×75 in.
2×6—20 ft.
  A 2 78 in.   **B** 2 42 in.
1×2—20 ft.
  E 2 75 in.   **F** 2 39 in.
2×4—12 ft.
  G 3 39 in.
2×12—4 ft.
  I 1 39 in.
6-in. diameter posts—12 ft.
  C 2 21 in.   **D** 2 42 in.
Glue, paint or stain, foam mattress, and fabric.

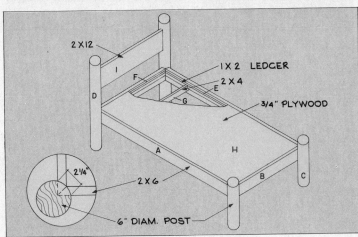

2 X 12
I
F
D
1 X 2 LEDGER
2 X 4
E
G
3/4" PLYWOOD
A
H
2 X 6
B
C
2¼"
6" DIAM. POST

TERRIFIC TABLES

Where can you put a brand-new, custom-made table? Just about anywhere! Perhaps you'd like a new coffee table for the den or living room. Or, maybe you'd just like to replace that nicked-up old wobbler that's been masquerading as your kitchen table.

Whatever your needs, get ready to forge ahead! The best part about building your own table is that it's so easy—just attach legs and a top!

This chapter features terrific table ideas that can work for you in all kinds of room situations. No matter which design you choose, you can adapt table length, width, or height to go with your other furniture pieces and to fit whatever space is available.

Choose a table style that will stand comfortably with your other furnishings. If your room has a modern look, you might want to build a sleek, low table with smooth lines and a glass or acrylic top. Or, if you lean toward a more traditionally styled room, remember that the look of real wood works well with just about any scheme.

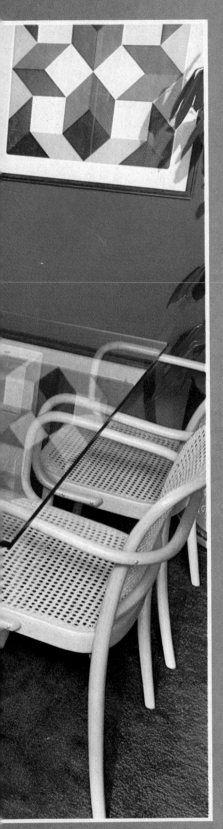

SEE-THROUGH TIMBER TABLE

Once you've bought your materials, it won't take long to stack up this table from 6x6 fir timbers and a top sheet of glass or acrylic. And, by layering on more or fewer 6x6s, you can build it to most any height. When assembling the base, lay the timbers one on top of the other, letting their weight keep them in place. Or, for a more permanent table, glue the base members together.

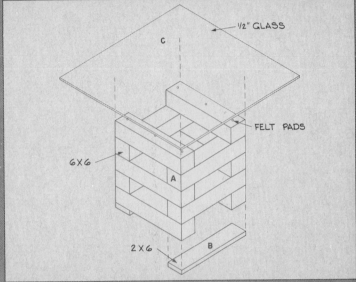

1 You can buy 6x6 timbers (A) for this table cut to size, or you can cut the lengths yourself from longer sections of lumber. In either case, accuracy is important since the edges of the table base should appear perfectly flush on all four sides.

2 Cut two sections from a fir 2x6 (B) for the bottom of the table base (see sketch). These will bring the table up dining table height.

3 Sand each 6x6 and 2x6 smooth. Stain and varnish the wood to any desired finish. Or if you prefer the natural look, simply apply a couple coats of polyurethane varnish.

4 Stack the 2x6s and 6x6s as shown in the sketch. As an option, glue pieces together as you stack them to form base.

5 Glue thin circular felt pads onto the top timbers to protect the glass or acrylic top.

6 Lift the top (C) onto the base. Measure to be sure that the top is located squarely on the timbers. If you decide on a glass top for the table, its weight probably will keep it in the correct position. For an acrylic top, use rubber rather than felt pads.

Materials (for a 48×48×29½-inch table):

6×6 fir—20 ft.
 A 10 24 in.
2×6 fir—4 ft.
 B 2 24 in.
½-inch seamed tempered glass or acrylic
 C 1 48×48 in.
Thin felt pads, glue (optional), and stain and varnish (optional).

ELEGANT OAK COFFEE TABLE

This unique coffee table gets its handsome surfaces from tongue-and-groove oak flooring. Smooth, mitered corners and professional construction techniques help make this table the equal of any commercially available piece of fine wood furniture. But you can build it for only a fraction of what it would cost from the showroom floor.

1 To build top, cut two strips (A) from 1x3 oak (use flooring with tongue-and-groove removed).

2 Butt together pieces of 1x3 flooring (B) to form top surface. Glue and nail on oak trim (A).

3 Glue and nail 1x3 spacers (C) followed by oak trim (D) to form underside support assembly (see sketch). Clamp until glue dries.

4 Cut a 45-degree edge along each end of tabletop assembly.

5 Repeat the above procedure to construct the two sides (E, F, G, H) of the table, mitering one end of each side panel.

6 Join the sides to top. Spread glue on all mitered surfaces. Press top to sides, matching corners and clamping. Crossbrace the sides with scrap lumber to keep the joints square. NOTE: For stronger joints, use splines or dowels (see page 88).

7 Drill pilot holes and nail joints together. Inset nails; fill holes.

8 Remove clamps and crossbraces. Face outside edges of sides and top with mitered oak strips (I, J). Add molding (K, L, M) as shown.

9 Sand, stain, and varnish table.

Materials (for a 25½×32×16-inch table):

1×3 tongue-and-groove oak flooring—78 ft.

B,F 24 24 in.	**A,I** 4 32 in.		
E,J,H 12 16 in.	**D** 2 29 in.		

1×3 pine or oak spacers—10 ft.

G 4 16 in.	**C** 2 30 in.

⅛-inch oak molding—16 ft.

M 2⅝×19 in.	**K** 2⅝×31 in.
L 4⅝×15 in.	

White wood glue, splines or dowels, wood filler, and stain and varnish.

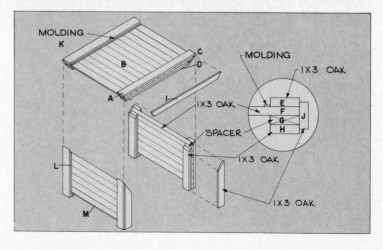

ORNAMENTAL
COFFEE
TABLE

Years ago, architects used wood carvings as ornamental trim around doors, windows, ceilings, and entryways. Now, the originals are collector's items. You can search out scraps of these intricate wood carvings at antique shops, auctions, or wherever old buildings are being cleared away. Then, use them as furniture decorations.

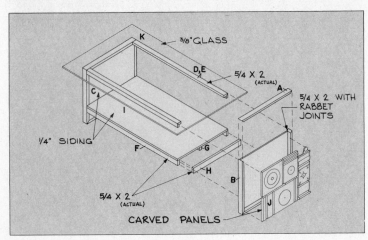

3/8" GLASS · 5/4 X 2 (ACTUAL) · D,E · K · C · 5/4 X 2 WITH RABBET JOINTS · A · I · 1/4" SIDING · F · G · H · B · J · 5/4 X 2 (ACTUAL)

CARVED PANELS

1 Construct side panels first. For each panel, cut a frame from 5/4x2-inch strips (A, B), mitering corners at a 45-degree angle. Make a ½-inch rabbet cut on the inside edge of each strip.

2 Using splines or dowels, join the mitered corners (see page 88). Glue and nail ¼-inch cedar siding (C) to each frame.

3 Next, glue and nail mitered 5/4x2s (D, E) together to use as the top stretchers (see sketch). Wait to install.

4 Construct a frame for the bottom shelf using 5/4x2 lumber for the side stretchers, center spine, and end pieces (F, G, H). Then, glue and nail on a piece of cedar siding (I) to form bottom.

5 Glue and nail bottom shelf assembly to side panels. Nail on top stretchers. For strength, use dowels at all joints.

6 Glue an assortment of carved panels (J) to the sides. Seal and finish the table.

7 Affix thin felt pads along top edge of side panels and stretchers and ease the ⅜-inch plate glass top (K) into place.

Materials (for a 46×28×18⅜-inch table):

5/4×2 cedar, pine, or fir—38 ft.

A	4	20 in.	**G**	1	33¾ in.
B	4	18 in.	**H**	2	17¾ in.
D,E,F	6	36 in.			

¼-in. rough cedar siding–½ sht.

C	2	18¾×16¾ in.
I	1	36×20 in.

⅜-in. seamed tempered plate glass

K	1	46×28 in.

Carved panels (J), glue, splines or dowels, wood filler, felt pads, and stain and varnish.

PARSONS-STYLE CONSOLE TABLE

Add a dash of class and a splash of panache to your decorating scheme with this easy-to-build console table. It's the perfect project to give new interest to the dead space in an entryway, behind a couch, or in a neglected corner. Use it with a small accent lamp to capture the beauty of your favorite knickknacks in the mirrored surface.

1 Cut panel (A) from ½-inch plywood to back mirror squares.

2 Attach two 2x2 nailers (B) to the top as shown. Then, frame the top with plywood strips butted together (C, D).

3 Glue and screw 3-inch-wide plywood verticals (E) to the 2x2s and top, one in each corner to form table legs (see sketch).

4 Cover horizontal 2x2 nailers with 3-inch-wide plywood strip (F) on both sides of tabletop. Glue and nail into place.

5 Line inside and outside of table's legs with panels (G, H).

6 Using white glue, cover table with vinyl fabric. Stretch tight enough to remove wrinkles (it will shrink slightly as it dries). Glue on zebrawood strips on each side of table (I).

7 Either just position the tiles or apply tile adhesive to the top and press mirror tiles (J) into place.

NOTE: For a different effect and an extra-tough top, consider using plastic laminate.

Materials (for a 54×18⅛×36-inch table):

½-inch plywood—1½ shts.

C	2	3×53 in.
F	2	3×47 in.
E	4	3×35½ in.
H	2	18⅛×36 in.
G	2	18⅛×32½ in.
A	1	17⅛×53 in.
D	2	2½×12⅛ in.

2×2 pine—10 ft.

B	2	53 in.

½-inch zebrawood

I	2	1½×46 in.

Four 12×12-in. mirror tiles (J), tile adhesive, vinyl fabric, white wood glue, and screws and nails.

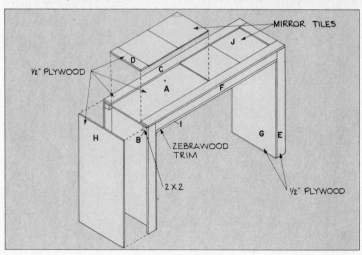

COFFEE TABLE HIDEAWAY

Somebody tucked their stereo and record albums inside this handy tabletop storage unit . . . and it works just great! But this project is also ideal for many other practical applications—like hiding bar supplies or housing a mini sewing center. Decorative wood shapes camouflage two swing-out lid supports, so you don't sacrifice surface space when the unit is open.

1 Cut out side (A, G), bottom (B), top (C), and divider (D) panels from ½-inch plywood.
2 Cut ½-inch notches 3 inches long in side panels (A) as shown. Then, construct the box-like storage area, using simple butt joints. Use glue and screws or nails to assemble.
3 Attach divider (D) as shown. Wait to install top panels.
4 Cut various plywood shapes (E), paint them different colors, and allow to dry.
5 Paint the box and top panels and allow to dry.
6 Glue and nail the plywood shapes to the sides of the box unit as shown. Attach the flip-out top supports (F) with butt hinges.
7 Attach the two long top panels (C) to the box with butt hinges.

Materials (for the unit shown):

½-inch birch plywood—1 sht.
 C 2 9×36 in. **A** 2 17×12 in.
 B 1 17×35 in. **G** 2 12×36 in.
 D 1 17×11½ in.
Miscellaneous plywood shapes
E,F each 11 in. high
Eight butt hinges, glue, screws, nails, and paint.

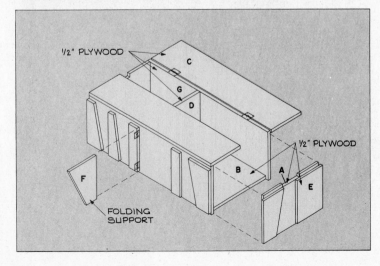

HEFTY REDWOOD COFFEE TABLE

This low-slung table is an outstanding example of sturdy furniture construction. And the assembly is just a leisurely afternoon's project, with final varnishing taking an hour or so on following days. When you're done, you'll find that for very few dollars you've crafted a beautiful table that's the match of any from the bench of a master woodworker!

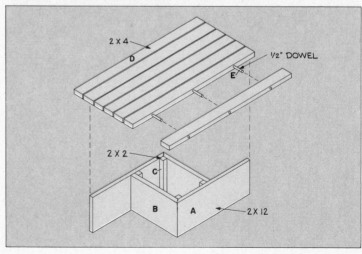

1 First build the modified box-type base from redwood 2x12s (A, B). Use butt joints, and glue and nail in place.

2 Reinforce corner base joints with 2x2 blocking strips (C) as shown. Glue and nail into place.

3 Construct the top from redwood 2x4s (D). Cut the pieces to size; then drill three ½-inch holes in identical locations on each 2x4. Sand each board smooth and stain. Follow with three coats of varnish.

4 Sand, stain, and varnish base.

5 Stain ½-inch dowels (E). When dry, insert a dowel into each hole in the first top plank. Glue into place.

6 One after another, slide 2x4s into position to form tabletop. Glue each one to dowels, leaving ¼-inch space between.

7 After glue is dry, cut off any excess dowel flush with the tabletop. Sand, stain, and varnish the exposed dowel ends to match the rest of the table.

8 To permanently attach the tabletop to the base, invert both pieces on the floor. Then screw angle braces between tabletop and each corner 2x2 on base.

Materials (for a 48×26×13-inch table):

2×12 redwood—8 ft.
  A 2 28 in.   **B** 2 18 in.
2×4 redwood—30 ft.
  D 7 48 in.
2×2 redwood—4 ft.
  C 4 11½ in.
½-inch dowel—8 ft.
  E 3 28 in.
Glue, four angle braces and screws, stain, and varnish.

TIP-PROOF TRESTLE TABLE

Solid construction makes this handsome trestle table unbeatable for standing up to rugged use. You'll think it's attractive enough to be the family dining table, yet it's so inexpensive to build, it makes a great play or study table for the kids. Seal it with a polyurethane varnish to protect its natural wood beauty year after year.

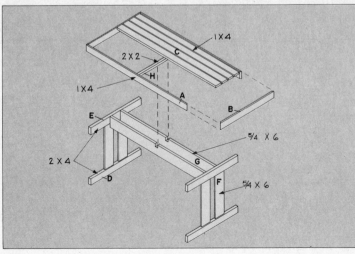

1 Start by building the tabletop frame. Miter 1x4s (A, B) at a 45-degree angle. Apply an even coat of glue to mitered surfaces.
2 Clamp. Check to see that frame is square. Drive two nails into corner joints. Let glue dry.
3 Cut 1x4 planks (C) to size for tabletop. Set aside.
4 Cut 2x4 legs (D, E) and 5/4x6 uprights (F) to size. Join each upright to top and bottom 2x4s with ½-inch dowels (two per joint). Glue, clamp, and let dry.
5 Cut 5/4x6 stretchers (G) to size. Notch center of each stretcher to allow for 2x2 nailer.
6 Sand, stain, and varnish all pieces for the table.
7 When pieces are dry, assemble table. Glue and screw 5/4x6 stretchers into place between the table legs. Nail and glue leg assembly to tabletop frame, butting against inside of frame and allowing a ¾-inch recess for top planks. Glue and nail on 2x2 crosspiece (H).
8 Nail on top planks (C), spacing ¼ inch apart. Fill nail holes.

Materials (60×31¾-inch table):
2×4 fir or clear pine—10 ft.
  E,D 4 30¼ in.
5/4×6 fir or clear pine—10 ft.
  G 2 55½ in.
5/4×6 fir or clear pine—8 ft.
  F 4 22¼ in.
1×4 fir or clear pine—66 ft.
  A 2 60 in. **B** 2 31¾ in.
  C 8 58½ in.
½-inch dowel—2 ft.
  16 1½ in.
2×2 fir or clear pine—4 ft.
  H 1 30¼ in.
Glue, screws, stain, and varnish.

SKYLIGHT TERRARIUM TABLE

Here's your chance to show off your wood craftsmanship *and* your green thumb . . . all in a build-it-from-scratch project. It's easy when you knock together this conversation-provoking table. The version shown is a coffee table design, but by modifying the dimensions slightly, you can make it a great dining table with a permanent centerpiece.

1 Build a frame of 1x4s for the tabletop assembly. Start by butting 1x4s (A, B) together to form the rectangular outer frame; glue and screw together.

2 Screw 1x4 crosspieces (C) into the frame as shown. Between the 1x4s at the center of the table, leave an open area just large enough for your planter box.

3 Build the planter from ½-inch plywood. Cut out the four sides (D) and the bottom (E); glue and nail together using butt joints.

4 Cut 1x4s to form top planks (F, G). Wait to install.

5 Stain and varnish tabletop pieces. When dry, treat planter box with waterproofing fiberglass resin or penta. Let dry.

6 Slide the planter box into the 1x4 tabletop frame, positioning sides of the planter flush with adjoining 1x4s. Screw into place as shown.

7 Build the two leg assemblies by sandwiching 1x4 crosspieces (H) between 1x4 uprights (I) as shown. Stain and varnish after bolting together as shown.

8 Slide each leg assembly into tabletop frame at desired locations. Screw legs to frame, countersinking screwheads.

9 Screw on top planks, (F, G) butting together as shown. Countersink screws.

10 Start a terrarium in the planter. Spread a thin layer of charcoal across the bottom of the planter; follow with a ½-inch layer of sand. Add 2 inches of potting soil and carefully set in your favorite terrarium plants. Cover with glass top (notch glass for easy removal).

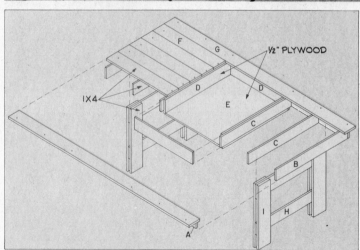

Materials (for a 54×24½×16¾-inch table):

1×4 fir or pine—66 ft.

I 10	16 in.	**G** 2	54 in.
B,C,H 10	20 in.	**A** 2	48 in.
F 8	18 in.		

½-inch plywood—½ sht.

D 4 5×18 in.
E 1 18×19½ in.

¼-inch glass top for terrarium
1 17¼×17¾ in.

Nuts and bolts, screws, glue, fiberglass resin or penta, and stain and varnish.

LATTICE-TOP PLANTER TABLE

On a patio, deck, or in front of a sunny bay window, this long, low table is poised for a proliferation of plants. The open latticework structure allows air to healthfully circulate around your green potted friends. And because it's built from redwood, this table can weather sun and rain, as well as a few inadvertent spills at watering time.

1 Build the frame for the tabletop by gluing and nailing together 1x3s (A, B) with butt joints.
2 Screw and glue 2x2 legs (C) to the frame, recessing them ¾-inch below the top of the frame.
3 Glue and nail 1x2 ledgers (D) to the inside of the two long frame members, ¾ inch below the top edge of the 1x3s.
4 Follow with the short 1x2 strips (E) to form the lattice top. Space evenly, glue, and nail.
5 If desired, leave the redwood natural. Or, sand and stain the table to match its surroundings. NOTE: If you're putting this planter in front of a window, you can adapt the height to give your plants maximum light exposure. Just add a few inches to the length of the legs.

Materials (for a 96×15½×14-inch table):

1×3 redwood—20 ft.
 A 2 94½ in. **B** 2 15½ in.
1×2 redwood—70 ft.
 E 43 14 in. **D** 4 45 in.
2×2 redwood—8 ft.
 C 6 13¼ in.
Galvanized screws and nails, glue, and stain (optional).

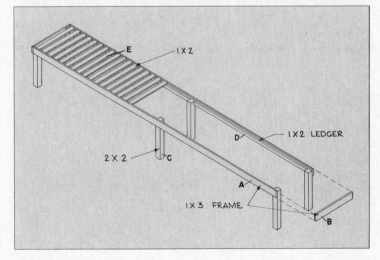

MIRRORED BUFFET / CURIO SHELF

We all need little conveniences that help us save time—ones that let us squeeze more hours of enjoyment out of the day.

So, take a look at the exciting projects in this chapter. They're designed to do just that!

You'll find instructions and plans for some stylish, specialized storage . . . a roll-away sewing center . . . double-duty desks . . . and even a multipurpose serving bar.

A professional furniture maker will tell you that the inner structure of most pieces—the frame—is basically simple. The real secret to building beautiful furniture is careful application of the finishing touches.

That's true for the furniture you build yourself, too. So if you're fairly new at this rewarding, relaxing hobby, take a few minutes to read through the "basics" section at the back of this book. You'll find all the information you need to achieve perfect results.

Then, just choose a project that suits you and start in. Build the activity center that will add real convenience and enjoyment to your life!

ROLL-AWAY SEWING CENTER

This portable sewing center doubles as a roomy, wall-hugging bedroom chest. Roll it away from the wall, and it swings into action as a self-contained sewing table with a flip-up top. Use plastic laminate for a durable working surface, and paint or antique the base to harmonize with your bedroom decor.

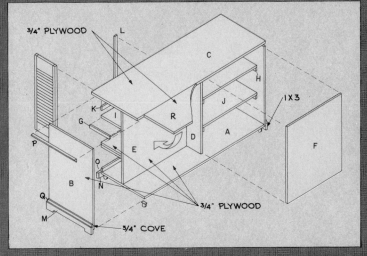

1 Cut out and assemble plywood bottom (A), sides (B), and top (C).

2 Glue and screw vertical dividers (D, E) into box at right angles as shown. Attach back (F).

3 Install 1x2 ledgers (G, H) as supports; mount shelves (I, J).

4 On the front of the unit, face inside edge of the top and bottom and exposed edge of the center divider (D) with 1x2 strips (K, L) to form the frame for the shutter doors.

5 Install casters. Cut out 1x3 skirting (M, N) to hide casters (see sketch). Add cove molding (O, P, Q).

6 Paint the unit. Separately, paint shutter doors. When dry, install doors and fasten on knobs.

7 Cut out drop leaf (R). Install plastic laminate on top sections.

8 Attach drop leaf with piano hinge. Add collapsible brackets as shown.

Materials (for an 18×48×30-inch chest):

¾-inch plywood—1½ shts.

B	2	18×27¼ in.
D	1	15×26½ in.
R	1	12×45 in.
I	2	8×22½ in.
F	1	26½×22½ in.
A	1	18×45 in.
C	1	18×48 in.
E	1	26½×22½ in.
J	2	15×21¾ in.

1×3 pine or fir—8 ft.

M	2	18¾ in.
N	1	48 in.

1×2 pine or fir—18 ft.

G	4	8 in.	H	4	15 in.
K	2	45 in.	L	1	23½ in.

¾-inch cove trim—16 ft.

O	2	48 in.	Q	2	18¾ in.
P	2	18 in.			

¾-inch shutter doors

4   10⅞×23½ in.

Casters, knobs, collapsible brackets, plastic laminate and adhesive, piano and butt hinges, screws, and glue.

MIRRORED BUFFET/ CURIO SHELF

As a storage area for your fine books and treasured collectibles, this unusual, modernistic shelving unit can't be beat. But, it's more than that! You can also put it to work as a strategically placed buffet server. Durable plastic laminate makes the top safe to serve from. And when it's not in use, leave the sliding doors open for a pleasing display.

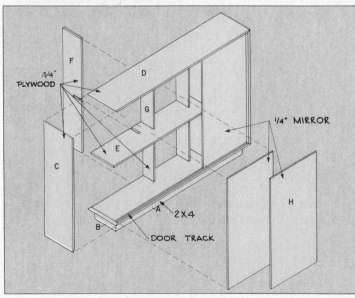

1 Build a rectangular base for the shelf unit from 2x4s (A, B). Miter corners; glue and nail together.

2 Construct outer shell of unit from ¾-inch plywood (C,D). Miter ends of boards as shown. Then after drilling pilot holes, glue and nail together. Cut two lengths of door track to size, then nail or screw them to the top and bottom panels (D).

3 Cut slots in the plywood center shelf (E) for edge cross lap joints. Install shelf.

4 Construct the vertical dividers (F, G) by cutting slots for cross lap joints. Glue each divider to shelf and frame.

5 Paint entire unit. Or, if desired, cover with vinyl fabric.

6 Insert ¼-inch glass panels (H) into door tracks.

7 Apply plastic laminate to top. NOTE: This shelf unit is designed without a back to transmit light when doors are open. If desired, you can enclose the back with ½-inch plywood.

Materials (for an 16×54×42-inch unit):

¾-inch plywood—1½ shts.
C 2 16×38½ in.
D 2 16×54 in.
E 1 14×52½ in.
F 2 14×37 in.
G 2 8×37 in.
2×4 pine or fir— 12 ft.
A 2 50 in.
B 2 12 in.
Glass doors (¼ in. thick)
H 3 18¼×36⅝ in.
Plastic laminate and adhesive, paint or vinyl fabric, screws, nails, sliding door track, and glue.

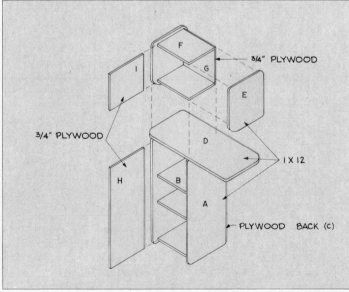

ONE-ARMED TELEPHONE STAND

1 To build the lower storage compartment, round corners off two sections of 1x12 sides (A).

2 Cut out 1x10 shelves (B). Attach sides to shelves with glue and countersunk screws. Plug holes with dowels. Glue and screw on back (C).

3 Cut a 1x12 to form the extended telephone shelf (D), rounding corners. Screw onto base unit, countersinking screws flush.

4 Build the upper storage compartment with sections of 1x12 to form sides (E). Round corners.

5 Cut out 1x10 shelves (F) and attach to sides. Countersink screws, plugging holes with dowel pieces. Glue and screw on back panel (G).

6 If desired, attach upper storage compartment to telephone shelf with dowels.

7 Paint or stain unit.

8 Cut out cabinet doors (H, I) per materials list. Paint or stain inside of doors; apply plastic laminate to outside surfaces.

9 Hang doors, using butt hinges. Add catches and knobs.

Materials (11¼×30×44-in. stand):

1×12 pine or fir—10 ft.
E	2	14 in.	**D** 1	30 in.
A	2	29¼ in.		

1×10 pine or fir—8 ft.
B,F 5 15 in.

¾-inch plywood—1 sht.
C	1	15×27¾ in.
G	1	12½×15 in.
I	1	12½×14¾ in.
H	1	14¾×27¾ in.

Wood dowels, plastic laminate and adhesive, doorknobs and catches, butt hinges, paint or stain, varnish, screws, and glue.

PLATFORM BED AND DESK ENSEMBLE

Children, students, apartment dwellers, and just about anyone will appreciate the space-saving utility of this desk and bed arrangement. It's a great addition to that extra bedroom, and best of all, it's a snap to build. Fashion the desk from two filing cabinets, a prebuilt drawer system, and a butcher-block top. Then, assemble the bed according to the instructions below, and you're in business.

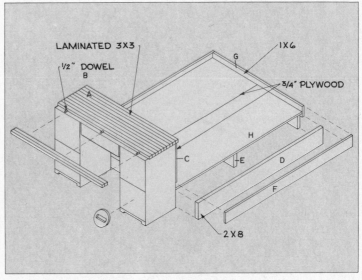

1 To build the butcher-block desk top, drill three evenly spaced holes in identical 2x2 boards (A). Apply glue and insert ½-inch dowels (B). Trim off excess dowel flush. Plane and sand top smooth. Seal, stain, and varnish.

2 When dry, screw top to two metal or plastic filing cabinets. Install prebuilt center drawer system by rigging to underside of top. Paint drawer and file cabinets. If desired, attach decorative drawer pulls as shown.

3 Attach desk back/headboard (C).

4 Build the bed frame from 2x8 supports (D, E) and 1x6 framing members (F, G). First, butt 2x8s together and glue and screw into place (see sketch).

5 Face 2x8s with 1x6s to form mattress frame as shown. Attach with screws and glue.

6 Cut two sections of ¾-inch plywood to form mattress platform (H). Insert onto 2x8 supports; screw into place.

7 Paint bed frame and headboard. Attach frame to desk by screwing together.

Materials (for unit shown):

3×3 maple—60 ft.
  A 12 54 in.
¾-inch plywood—2 shts.
  H 2 27×75 in.   **C** 1 22×54 in.
2×8 pine or fir—34 ft.
  D 2 75 in.   **E** 3 51 in.
1×6 pine or fir—28 ft.
  F 2 76½ in.   **G** 2 54 in.
½-in. wood dowel—6 ft.
  B 3 18½ in.
Two metal or plastic filing cabinets, one prebuilt drawer system, glue, screws, paint, stain, varnish, and drawer pulls (optional).

BUTCHER-BLOCK PUSHCART

If your dining table gets too crowded with serving dishes every now and then, here's a smart solution. Park this easy-rolling cart close-by to take care of the mealtime clut-ter. The butcher-block top is a real boon for preparing sparkling fresh salads or other treats right at tableside. And between meals, the cart makes a great portable bar.

1 Cut four lengths of 5/4x2 to serve as uprights (A). Also cut all 5/4x2 framing members shown (miter corners as necessary).

2 Make ¼-inch rabbet cuts in lower frame (D, E, F) and dado cuts in uprights for bottom shelf.

3 Assemble cart frame, using 1½-inch dowels (one per joint) and gluing together wherever 5/4x2s join uprights. Glue and nail together only three sides of the mitered bottom shelf frame. (Insert 3-inch-long dowels completely through uprights to join shelf frame to uprights.)

4 Slide ¼-inch hardboard shelf (H) into rabbet cuts on shelf frame; glue and nail in place. Attach fourth side of frame (E).

5 To make top, drill holes in 5/4x2 pieces of lumber (I, J). Hide dowels by sinking holes only ½ inch deep into the end 5/4x2s.

6 Insert ½-inch dowels (K) and pull handle (L) into holes; glue top together. Attach top to cart with dowels or angle braces.

7 Stain and varnish cart. Install 2-inch ball-type stem casters.

Materials (for project shown):

5/4×2 walnut and/or maple—82 ft.

I	4	34 in.	**J**	16	30 in.
A	4	24¾ in.	**B,D**	4	20 in.
C	2	13½ in.	**E,G**	4	16 in.
F	4	5¾ in.		

¼-inch hardboard—½ sht.

H	1	16½×33¾ in.

½-inch dowel—8 ft.

K	2	17 in.	16	1½ in.
	4	3 in.		

¾-inch dowel

L	1	17 in.

Casters, stain, varnish, and glue.

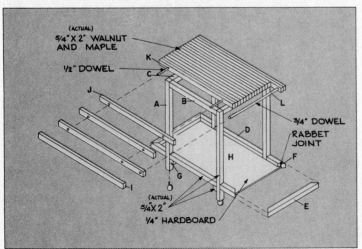

(ACTUAL) 5/4" X 2" WALNUT AND MAPLE

½" DOWEL

¾" DOWEL

RABBET JOINT

(ACTUAL) 5/4" X 2"

¼" HARDBOARD

PLYWOOD STUDY DESK

Need somewhere to sit down and get a lot of work done? Then pull up a chair to this good-looking study desk. In the kitchen, it's a great place to sit and figure out the grocery list. Left unfinished and built a little taller, it serves as a light-duty workbench. The hardest part about building this desk is waiting for the paint to dry so you can use it!

1 Assemble shelf box first. Cut pieces of ¾-inch plywood to form sides (A), shelves (B), and back (C). Make dado cuts in sides to support shelves. Glue and screw sides (A) and back (C) of shelf unit together.

2 Slip shelves (B) into dado cuts; glue and screw into place. NOTE: for neatest appearance, countersink all screws and fill holes.

3 Cut top (D) and tall side (E) from ¾-inch plywood. Glue and screw top to shelving unit; then, attach side (E) to top.

4 Glue and screw a 2x2 blocking strip (F) to the underside of top. Attach plywood backboard (G) to desktop and 2x2 strip.

5 Add the triangular gusset (H) for strength. Glue and screw a plywood facing plate (I) to shelf unit as shown. NOTE: If desired, build a drawer or an additional shelf into the desk in place of the facing plate. See instructions for building drawers on page 92.

6 Paint entire unit. When dry, glue plastic laminate to top.

Materials (for a 24×60×30-inch desk):

¾-inch plywood—2 shts.

D	1	59¼×23¼ in.
E	1	36×24 in.
C	1	24×18 in.
B	3	22½×18½ in.
G	1	59¼×12 in.
A	2	23¼×29¼ in
I	1	6×18 in.
H	1	6-in. triangular gusset

2×2 pine or fir—4 ft.

F	1	39¾ in.

Plastic laminate and adhesive, wood filler, screws, and glue.

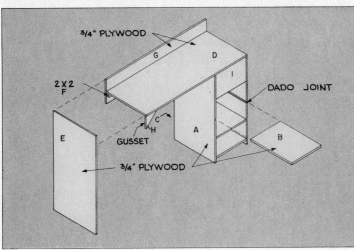

¾" PLYWOOD

2 × 2
F

DADO JOINT

GUSSET

¾" PLYWOOD

MULTIPURPOSE ISLAND COUNTER

Short on kitchen counter and storage space? Then try this project for size. With a flip of the top and a turn of the wrist, it becomes a double-wide serving center. Complete with drawers and cupboard for storing lots of supplies, this unique countertop unit is truly a versatile home project. Finish it with paneling to match the rest of your cabinetry.

1 Build the kickboard base from 1x3s (A, B) butted together (see sketch). Cut back (C), bottom (D), sides (E, F), tops (G, H, I), shelves (J), and dividers (K, L, M) from ¾-inch plywood.

2 Glue and screw together sides, back, bottom, and dividers as shown (brace horizontal divider (K) with 1x2 ledgers). Install ledgers and shelves (J) in small storage area.

3 Fit sub-top (G) into place. Drill hole for carriage bolt.

4 Face outside of unit with paneling.

5 Assemble drawers, making ¼-inch rabbet cuts for bottoms (N) and butting sides (O), backs (P), and fronts (Q). Face with paneling.

6 Attach metal drawer guides.

7 Install plastic laminate on top sections (H, I). Join tops with piano hinge.

8 Install carriage bolt pivot.

9 Cut out sliding doors (R); face with paneling. Install sliding door guides and doors.

Materials (24×48×30-inch unit):

¾-inch plywood—3½ shts.

E	2	24×26 in.
M	1	24×25¼ in.
C	1	26×36 in.
H,I	2	24×48 in.
L	1	5½×23¼ in.
D	1	23¼×46½ in.
G,K	2	23¼×36 in
J	2	23¼×9¾ in.
F	1	9¾×25¼ in.

¼-inch plywood—½ sht.

R	2	18×19 in.

½-inch plywood—1 sht.

Q	2	17½×5¼ in.
P	2	15⅝× 5¼ in.

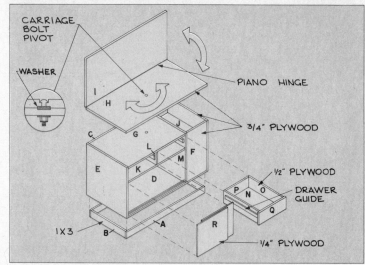

O	2	20×5¼ in.
N	2	16⅛×19¾ in.

⅛-inch paneling—1½ shts.

1×3 pine or fir—12 ft.

A	2 44 in.	B 2 18½ in.

1×2 pine or fir ledgers—12 ft.
6 22 in.

Plastic laminate and adhesive, carriage bolt and hardware, drawer and door guides, knobs, screws, glue.

DOUBLE-DUTY SERVING BAR

Breakfast bar, party bar, or serving counter? Whatever you call it, this easy furniture project works overtime. Remove the legs and slip off the top for a ready-made storage shelf. Or, turn the legless unit on its side and it's an instant bookshelf and stereo stand.

1 Build the box section from ¾-inch plywood. Cut an identical top (A), bottom (B), and center shelf (C); then, cut dividers (D).

2 Join center shelf (C) and two vertical dividers (D) with edge cross lap joints. Glue and screw on top and bottom pieces (A, B).

3 Nail 1x4 slats (E) onto frame, butting one against the next. Hide nailheads; fill holes.

4 Attach legs by drilling holes for hanger bolts, inserting T-nuts, and screwing together.

5 Cut out plywood bar top (F).

6 Install plastic laminate onto bar top.

7 Frame bar top with 1x2s (G, H), mitering corners and gluing and nailing together.

8 Paint or stain and varnish all exposed wood surfaces.

Materials 21½×48×42-inch bar):

¾-inch plywood—1 sht.
A,B,C 3 14¾×40½ in.
   D 2 14¾×25¾ in.
   F 1 20×46½ in.
1×4 pine or fir—50 ft.
   E 20 27¼ in.
1×2 pine or fir—12 ft.
   G 2 48 in. **H** 2 21½ in.
4 14-inch table legs
Plastic laminate and adhesive, ¼-inch T-nuts and hanger bolts, glue, screws, and nails.

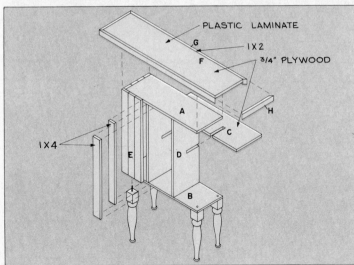

PLASTIC LAMINATE
1 X 2
G
F
¾" PLYWOOD
A
H
C
1 X 4
E
D
B

FURNITURE BY THE ROOMFUL

Beware . . . once you get started building your own furniture, you'll find that one good project leads to another. So why fight it? Go ahead and tackle something ambitious—like a whole roomful of furniture.

Start by building the projects you need most, such as a bed frame and headboard for that extra bedroom . . . a pair of easy chairs for the living room . . . or a work center for your utility room. Then, one by one, add matching accessories until you have a wall-to-wall designer's collection of unique, custom-made furniture.

If you like, create the finishing touches for your do-it-yourself furnishings by making your own rugs, cushions, and drapes. Can you think of a more practical way to inject touches of your personality into your decor?

This chapter shows four rooms furnished almost entirely with home-built projects—a living room, a multipurpose den, a dining area, and a bedroom. There are lots of ideas—so feel free to use these projects singly as well as in the room groupings shown.

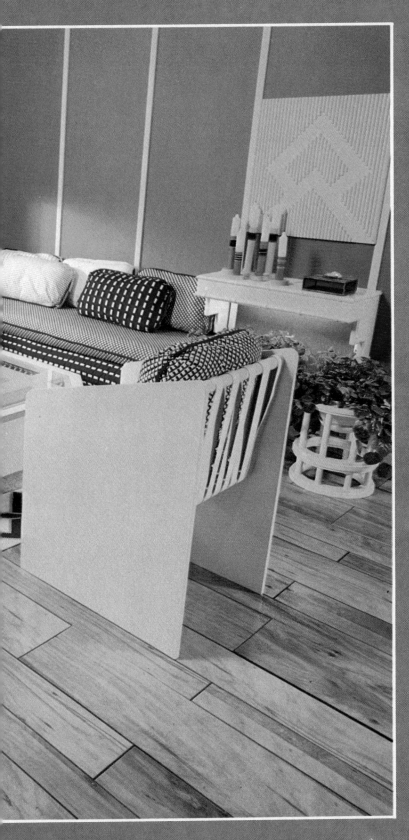

LIVELY LIVING ROOM ARRANGEMENT

It's no accident that this arrangement of table, chairs, plant stands, and desk complement each other and blend perfectly with the clean, modern lines of this attractive living room. Each of these projects is equally at home in a den or family room, too. Match them with your existing color scheme to add decorating impact and practicality to your room furnishings.

CHAIRS (sketch on page 36)
1 Make a pattern and cut out two sides (A) for each chair from ¾-inch plywood. Sides are 24 inches high at front, and 30 inches at back. Round corners.
2 Locate and drill 1¼-inch holes ½ inch deep to accommodate seat and back support dowels (B). Cut dowels to size; glue and nail into holes on one of the sides. Inset nails and fill holes.
3 If desired, fill plywood edges. Paint sides and dowels.
4 Cut 1½-inch-wide strips of canvas (C) and sew ends to form loops. Slip ends of loops onto dowels, running each loop around underside of back bottom dowel.
5 Glue and nail second side to dowels. Add cushions.

Materials (for one chair):
¾-inch birch plywood—1 sht.
  A 2 30×30 in. cut to shape shown
1¼-inch dowel—6 ft.
  B 3 19½ in.
Six strips of 1½-inch-wide canvas (**C**), wood filler, nails, glue; and paint.

(continued)

LIVELY LIVING ROOM ARRANGEMENT

(continued)

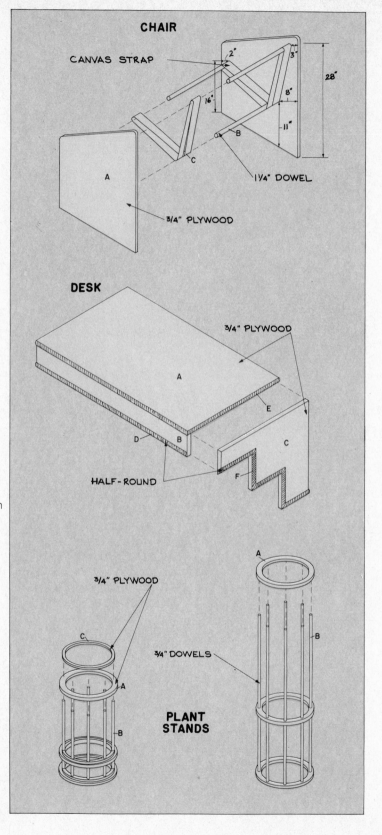

CHAIR

CANVAS STRAP

2"
3"
28"
16"
8"
11"
A
B
C
1¼" DOWEL
¾" PLYWOOD

DESK

¾" PLYWOOD
A
E
D
B
C
F
HALF-ROUND

¾" PLYWOOD
C
A
B
¾" DOWELS
A
B
PLANT STANDS

DESK

1 Cut top (A) and front plate (B) for desk from ¾-inch plywood. Make pattern and cut two identical plywood sides (C).

2 Glue and screw sides, top, and front together using butt joints. Set screwheads flush.

3 Trim edges with split bamboo molding (D, E, F), mitering corners and gluing into place.

4 Paint and allow to dry. NOTE: For a more serviceable top surface, apply plastic laminate. If desired, add vinyl edge strips.

5 Position desk top 29 inches from floor. Locate studs and anchor to wall with shelf brackets.

Materials (for a 31×18½×29-inch desk):

¾-inch birch plywood—1 sht.
  A 1 18×30 in. **B** 1 28½×3¼ in
  C 2 17¼×15¼ in.
½-inch round split bamboo trim
  D 2 31 in.   **E** 2 18½ in.
  F 10 6½ in.
Shelf brackets, paint, screws, and glue.

PLANT STAND

1 Cut circular rings (A) from ¾-inch plywood. NOTE: If desired, also cut circular trim rings (C) and glue to rings (A).

2 Determine desired height of stand. Cut ¾-inch dowel to size.

3 Drill eight evenly spaced ¾-inch holes completely through center rings. Using the drilled ring as a pattern, drill ½-inch-deep holes in top and bottom rings.

4 Insert dowels and glue center rings into position. Follow by gluing on top and bottom rings.

(continued)

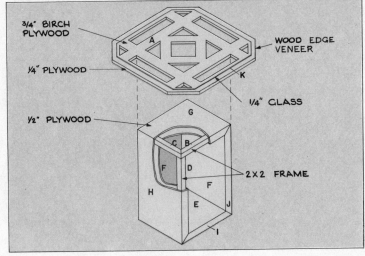

2 Paint top desired color; trim edge with vinyl veneer.

3 Build a frame for the base from 2x2s (B, C, D) cut to size and butted together with glue and nails.

4 Cut pieces of ½-inch plywood (E, F) to face inside of 2x2 frame. Miter plywood edges. Glue and nail into place. Inset nailheads and fill holes.

5 Face outside of frame with pieces of plywood (G, H). Miter edges; glue and nail onto 2x2s. Inset nailheads and fill holes.

6 Miter edges of 2½-inch-wide plywood strips (I, J) and glue and nail into place. Sink nails.

7 Paint base to match top.

8 Order ¼-inch glass (K) cut to shape of tabletop. Position it.

Materials (for a 40½×34½ ×30-inch dining table or a 40½ ×34½×16-inch coffee table):

¾-inch birch plywood—½ sht.
  A 1 40½×34½ in. cut to shape shown

½-inch birch plywood—1 sht.
  G 2 15×20 in.
  E 2 15×16 in.
  I 4 2½×20 in.
  J 4 2½×29 in.
  H 2 15×29 in.
  F 2 15×26 in.

¼-inch birch plywood
Enough to frame the outer edge of the top surface.

2×2 pine or fir—22 ft.
  D 4 25 in.
  B 4 19 in.
  C 4 14 in.

¼-inch glass with seamed edges
  K 1 Cut to fit within the frame

Wood edge veneer, wood filler, nails, glue, and paint.

5 Paint stand desired color.

Materials (for one plant stand):

¾-inch birch plywood—¼ sht.
  A 3 rings, 12-inch out. diam., 10-inch in. diam.
  C 3 rings, 11½-inch out. diam., 10-inch in. diam. (optional)

¾-inch dowel
  B Eight pieces of equal length
Paint and glue.

TABLE

NOTE: This versatile table serves a double function. Stand the base on end for a dining-height table. Or, lay the base lengthwise for a low coffee table.

1 Make a pattern and cut out tabletop shape (A) from a piece of ¾-inch plywood (see sketch). Frame the outer edge of the top surface with ¼-inch plywood.

DYNAMIC DEN

Right now, this den is a quiet room for reading and relaxing. But at other times, it hums with activity as a multipurpose work center. Just about every available inch of space has a function: seating, work surface, shelving, or storage. So much beauty and utility—yet you'll find the furniture is amazingly easy to build!

WORK CENTER

1 Construct lower desk top/storage areas first..Cut out top sections (A, B, C), sides (D, E), bottoms (F), and backs (G, H).

2 Building one section at a time, assemble sides, bottoms, and tops. Wait to install flip-open tops (C). Use butt joints, gluing and screwing pieces together and countersinking all screwheads. Fill holes with wood filler.

3 Screw and glue horizontal dividers (I) into place.

4 Next, build the two large drawer assemblies. Cut out sides (J), backs (K), and bottoms (L); make dado cuts in sides and backs to accommodate drawer bottoms. Assemble.

5 Cut out four drawer fronts (M), notching top of each as shown. Use two as false fronts for top-access storage areas. Glue and nail remaining two to drawers. Attach metal drawer guides to drawer assemblies and frame.

6 Install front plates (O) for desk section (cover with fabric, if desired). Glue and nail on 1x2 crosspieces (N) as shown.

7 Install drawer support (P). Assemble and attach center drawers (Q,R,S,T), using metal guides.

(continued)

DYNAMIC
DEN

(continued)

8 Paint entire unit. Separately, paint previously cut top sections (C). When dry, attach flip-up tops to top sections (A) with butt hinges.

9 Next, build upper shelf and rack areas. Cut out verticals for all sections (U, V). Drill three 3/8-inch-deep holes in verticals (U) for dowels; glue dowels (W) into place as shown.

10 Cut out shelves for remaining sections (X, Y). Working one section at a time, install shelves between verticals, gluing and screwing together.

11 Cut out back for center peg section (Z). Drill holes for 3/4-inch pegs; glue pegs into holes. Install peg section between shelf areas as shown.

12 Screw each shelf and rack assembly to base. For stability, screw shelf and rack uprights one to another.

13 Paint shelf and rack areas.

Materials (for a 28×96×80-inch work center):

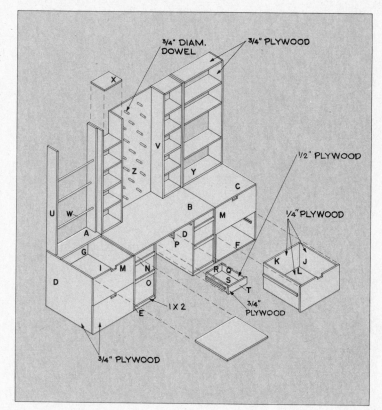

3/4-inch plywood—7 shts.

A	2	8×24 in.
B	1	28×48 in.
C	2	20×24 in.
K	2	20×14⅛ in.
P	1	4×20 in.
U	2	6×50 in.
X	12	8×10½ in.
Z	1	24×50 in.
D	6	27¼×29¼ in.
G	2	22½×29¼ in.
F,I	2	22½×26½ in.
L	2	20½×25½ in.
O	2	10½×29¼ in.
E	2	28×29¼ in.
M	4	24×14⅝ in.
T	2	12×4 in.

V	6	8×50 in.
Y	5	22½×8 in.
J	4	26×14⅛ in.
H	1	46½×29¼ in. (hidden)

1/2-inch plywood—1/2 sht.

Q	4	18×4 in.
R	2	9⅝×4 in.
S	2	10⅛×18¼ in.

1×2 pine—6 ft.

N	6	10½ in.

3/4-inch dowels—12 ft.

W	3	23¼ in.
	17	4 in. pegs

Drawer guides, butt hinges, screws, wood filler, glue, and paint.

END TABLE (sketch on next page)

1 Build U-shaped frame for table by butting 2x4s (A, B) together. Line inside and outside of 2x4 frame sections with plywood panels (C, D). Glue and screw pieces together. Countersink screwheads and fill holes.

2 Cover back of table with plywood panel (E). Cut U-shaped piece (F) to cover 2x4 frame at front of table.

3 Screw and glue on the top panel (G).

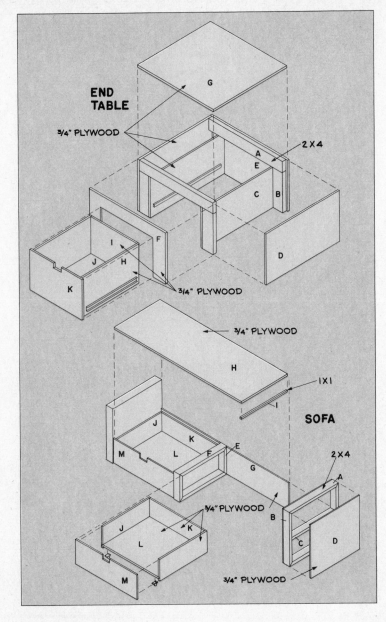

END TABLE

¾" PLYWOOD

2 X 4

¾" PLYWOOD

¾" PLYWOOD

SOFA

1 X 1

2 X 4

¾" PLYWOOD

¾" PLYWOOD

strength. Face inside of each frame assembly with plywood panels (D), notching panels to accommodate back of sofa.

2 Construct center support frame from mitered 2x4s (E, F).

3 Screw plywood back (G) to sofa arms and center support.

4 Cut plywood seat (H) to size. Screw and glue 1x1 ledgers (I) to underside of seat. Lower seat onto center frame and plywood back. Glue and screw into place. From underneath, screw seat to each sofa arm assembly by driving long screws through 1x1 ledgers (I) into plywood panel (D) and 2x4 crosspiece (C).

5 Construct caster-mounted drawers. Cut out sides (J) and back (K), making ⅜-inch-deep dado cuts to accommodate bottom (L). Glue and screw sides, back, and bottom together. Cut drawer front (M) to size and install. Screw on 1½-inch plate casters.

6 If desired, fill plywood edges. Paint all surfaces.

Materials (for an 80×30×15-inch sofa):

¾-inch plywood—4 shts.

D	4 27×30 in.	**H** 1 70×30 in.
M	2 33⅛×13¼ in.	
K	2 31⅝×12 in.	
J	4 28½×12 in.	
G	1 71½×14¼ in.	
L	2 28⅛×32⅜ in.	

2×4 pine—30 ft.

A	4 30 in.	**B,C** 6 27 in.
E	2 14¼ in.	**F** 2 29¼ in.

1×1 pine—6 ft.

I 2 28½ in.

Eight plate casters, wood filler, screws, glue, and paint.

4 Construct drawer by cutting out the sides (H), back (I), and bottom (J). Rabbet sides and back to accommodate bottom. Glue and screw together. Glue and screw on drawer front (K).

5 Paint table and drawer.

Materials (for a 30×30×18-inch table):

¾-inch plywood—2 shts.

C	2 13¾×28½ in.
D	2 17¼×28½ in.
E	1 17¼×30 in.
H	2 12¾×26 in.

J	1 18×25½ in.
I	1 12¾×17½ in.
K	1 12¾×19⅞ in.
G	1 30×30 in.
F	1 17¼×30 in. cut to shape shown

2×4 pine—12 ft.

A 2 28½ in.	**B** 4 13¾ in.

Metal drawer guides, wood filler, screws, glue, and paint.

SOFA

1 Build frame for sofa arms from mitered 2×4s (A, B). Nail and glue on 2×4 crosspieces (C) for

MODULAR DINING AREA

Here's how to furnish an entire dining/family room for little more than the cost of just four sheets of plywood. Cube-like stacking tables combine to form a neat corner bookshelf and display area. And the similarly styled seats and table are great for family meals, hobbies, or any activity requiring a sturdy, flat surface. Use two coats of a good interior enamel paint on all pieces for durability and easy cleanup.

DINING TABLE (sketch on page 44)

1 To build dining table, first make a frame for top from 1x4s (A,B). Glue and nail together; countersink nailheads and fill holes.

2 Cut out the top (C) from ¾-inch plywood. Fit top into 1x4 frame flush with top edge of 1x4s; glue and nail together. Countersink nailheads and fill holes.

3 Cut out slotted table legs (D, E) from ¾-inch plywood and glue together, using edge cross lap joints as shown (see sketch).

4 If desired, fill plywood edges. Paint top and legs. When dry, set top on legs. Attach top to legs using angle braces (optional).

Materials (for a 48×24×30-inch table):

¾-inch birch plywood—1½ shts.

C 1 22½×46½ in.
D 2 46½×29¼ in.
E 2 22½×29¼ in.

1x4 pine, fir, or birch—12 ft.

A 2 48 in. **B** 2 22½ in.

Angle braces (optional), wood filler, screws, glue, and paint.

(continued)

MODULAR DINING AREA

(continued)

SEATS

1 Form frame for seat cushion from 1x4s (F), mitering corners and joining with glue and nails. Cut out plywood top (G), position as shown, and glue and nail to frame. Countersink nailheads and fill holes.

2 Construct leg assembly from notched plywood pieces (H). Join with edge cross lap joints, gluing together.

3 Screw top to legs, countersinking screwheads flush.

4 Fill exposed plywood edges, if desired, and paint entire seat. Make or buy cushions to fit seat top (see instructions for making cushions on page 95).

Materials (19½ × 19½-inch seat):

¾-inch birch plywood—¼ sht.
  G 1 18×18 in.
  H 2 18×14 in.
1x4 pine, fir, or birch—8 ft.
  F 4 19½ in.
Wood filler, screws, nails, and glue.

STACKING TABLE

1 Cut top (I) from ¾-inch plywood.

2 Cut out slotted plywood legs (J); glue together with edge cross lap joints.

3 Glue and screw top to leg assembly, countersinking screwheads and filling holes.

4 If desired, fill plywood edges. Paint table.

Materials (for one 15×15×14¾-inch table):

¾-inch birch plywood—¼ sht.
  I 1 15×15 in.
  J 2 14×14 in.
Wood filler, screws, glue, and paint.

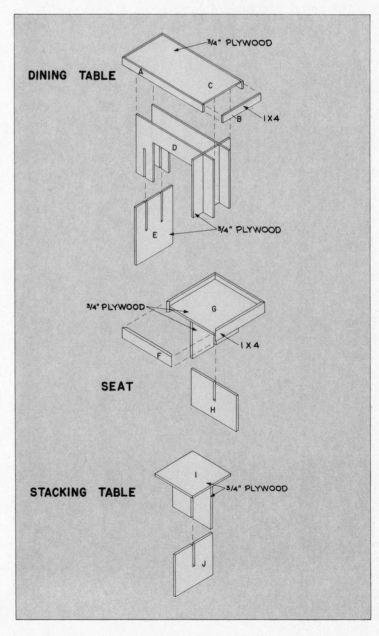

DINING TABLE

SEAT

STACKING TABLE

CHARMING CHILD'S BEDROOM

What youngster wouldn't love a setup like this specially built bedroom arrangement? Full of cubbyholes and cupboards for hoarding treasures, this practical furniture is constructed from rugged materials that make it just right for kids. For extra durability, apply plastic laminate to tops and finish wood surfaces with two coats of polyurethane varnish.

(continued)

CHARMING CHILD'S BEDROOM

(continued)

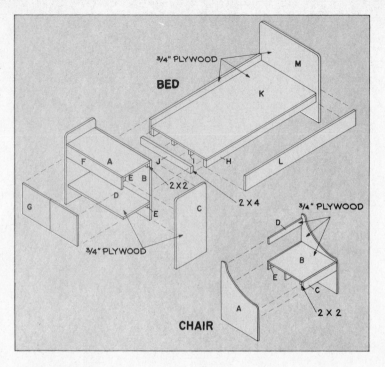

BED

¾" PLYWOOD

M

K

J I H L

2 × 2

2 × 4

F A

E B

D

G E

C

¾" PLYWOOD

¾" PLYWOOD

D

B

E

C

2 × 2

A

CHAIR

BED AND STORAGE UNIT

1 Cut out storage unit top (A), back (B), sides (C), and shelf (D). Round corners on sides as shown.
2 Using screws and glue, butt together sides, top, back, and shelf. Strengthen joints with 2x2 corner braces (E) as shown. Attach plywood front plate (F).
3 Cut out storage area doors (G). Wait to install.
4 To build bed frame, construct lower frame of 2x4s (H,I,J) butted together as shown. Fortify the frame by screwing an angle brace in each corner.
5 Nail plywood bedboard (K) to 2x4 frame. Follow with sideboards (L), gluing and screwing to 2x4 frame members. Inset screwheads and fill holes.
6 Cut out headboard (M), rounding corners as shown.
7 Position mattress frame at desired height from floor (support with scrap lumber while installing). Attach to storage area back (B) and headboard (M) with long screws. Countersink screwheads and fill holes.
8 Stain and varnish entire bed/storage unit. Separately, stain and varnish storage area doors (G). When doors are dry, install with butt hinges. Add magnetic catches.
9 Cover all exposed plywood edges with vinyl veneer.

Materials (for unit shown):
¾-inch plywood—2½ shts.
  M 1 40½×34 in.
  C 2 34×18 in.
  B 1 39×30 in.
  L 2 75×9 in.

  K 1 39×75 in.
A,D 2 39×17¼ in.
  G 2 19⅜×14 in.
  F 1 39×6¼ in.
2×4 pine or fir—28 ft.
  H 2 75 in. **I** 2 72 in.
  J 2 36 in.
2×2 pine or fir—10 ft.
  E 3 39 in.
Magnetic catches, four butt hinges, vinyl edge veneer, nails, screws, glue, stain, and varnish.

DESK CHAIR

1 Make pattern and cut out sides (A).
2 Cut out seat bottom (B), seat supports (C), and seat back (D).
3 Assemble chair with glue and screws. Strengthen seat supports with 2x2 corner braces (E). Inset screwheads and fill holes.
4 Stain and varnish. Cover plywood edges with vinyl veneer.

Materials (for 30-in.-high chair):
¾-inch plywood—1 sht.
  B 1 16×16 in. **D** 1 16×3 in.
  C 3 16×4¾ in.
  A 2 30×16 in. (cut to shape shown)
2×2 pine or fir—4 ft.
  E 2 16 in.
Vinyl edge veneer, screws, glue, stain, and varnish.

DESK

1 Cut out sides (A), top (B), front plate (C), and back plate (D). Round corners of sides as shown.
2 Assemble desk, screwing and gluing butt joints together.
3 Strengthen with 2x2 corner braces (E).
4 Stain and varnish all surfaces.
5 Cover all exposed plywood edges with vinyl veneer.

Materials (for a 42×18×30-inch desk):
¾-inch plywood—1 sht.
  A 2 18×32 in.
  B 1 16½×42 in.
  C 1 42×6¼ in.
  D 1 42×2¾ in.
2×2 pine or fir—8 ft.
  E 2 42 in.
Vinyl edge veneer, screws, glue, stain, and varnish.

MIRROR

1 Cut out plywood mirror frame (A), just smaller than mirror.
2 Drill holes for ¾-inch dowels. Glue dowels (B) into holes.
3 Stain and varnish frame. Allow to dry. Cover exposed plywood

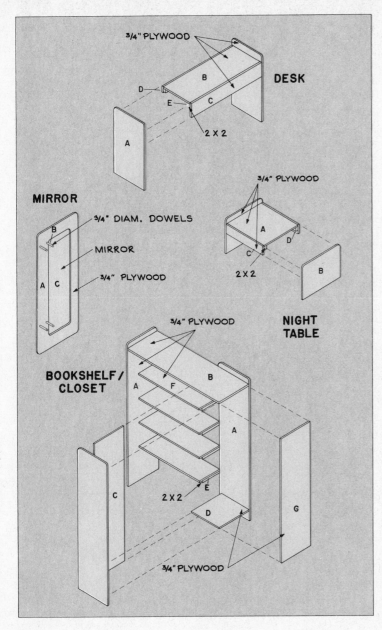

Materials (for a 22×23½×18-inch table):

¾-inch plywood—½ sht.
  A 1 16½×18 in.
  B 2 18×18 in.
  C 2 18×6¼ in.
2×2 pine or fir—4 ft.
  D 2 18 in.
Vinyl edge veneer, screws, glue, stain, and varnish.

BOOKSHELF/CLOSET

1 Cut out plywood sides (A) and top (B). Butt sides to top, gluing and screwing together.
2 Cut plywood divider (C) to size and install, butting against sides (A) and top. Glue and screw on closet bottom (D).
3 Attach 2x2 ledgers (E) to bookshelf sides (A,C) and lay shelves (F) on ledgers.
4 Cut out plywood closet door (G). Wait to install.
5 Stain and varnish unit. Separately, paint or stain closet door.
6 When door is dry, attach with butt hinges. Install handle and catches.
7 Face all exposed plywood edges with vinyl veneer.

Materials (for unit shown):

¾-inch plywood—3 shts.
  A 3 18×72 in.
  C 1 18×68 in.
  G 1 17⅞×67⅛ in.
  D 1 18×17¼ in.
  B 1 18×54 in.
  F 4 12×36 in.
2×2 pine or fir—8 ft.
  E 8 10 in.
Vinyl edge veneer, three butt hinges, door handle and catches, screws, glue, stain, paint (optional), and varnish.

edges with vinyl veneer.
4 Install rectangular mirror (C) with plastic or metal mirror fasteners. Hang mirror.

Materials (for a 24×48-inch mirror):

¾-inch plywood—¼ sht.
  A 1 24×48 in. (cut to shape shown)
¾-inch dowel—1 ft.
  B 4 2¾ in.
¼-inch mirror
  C 1 14×42 in.

Vinyl edge veneer, glue, mirror fasteners, stain, and varnish.

NIGHT TABLE

1 Cut out plywood top (A) and sides (B). Round corners of sides. Glue and screw together, adding 4-inch-wide stretchers (C).
2 Install corner braces (D) for strength.
3 Stain and varnish table.
4 Cover exposed plywood edges with vinyl veneer.

BEDS AND BOARDS

If searching for that perfect bedroom decorating idea is keeping you awake nights, the following seven projects should offer some relief. Several are suitable for furnishings throughout the house—lounges for the family or rec room, or guest-sleeping in the den.

The rest are designed to meet the special demands of your kids—sturdy, yet attractive, bunks and beds that can take every bit of rough-and-tumble action youngsters can dish out. There's even a charming crib that's sure to become a family heirloom.

Most of these designs accommodate standard-sized mattresses—39×75 inches for twin size, and 54×75 inches for a double mattress. You can cut foam slab mattresses to any size, though, so simply adjust the dimensions of the materials to make the size bed you need.

BUILDING-BLOCK BUNK

Bedtime won't be the usual hassle with this clean-looking bunk. It's styled after an arrangement of your kids' building blocks . . . but much sturdier, of course. An age-old wood joinery technique—doweled joints—is the secret to its solid construction.

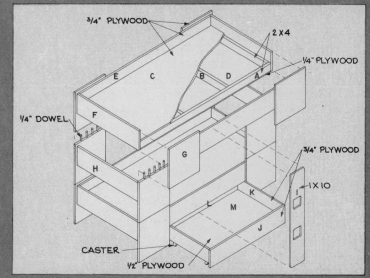

1 Build bed mattress frames of 2x4s (A, B) using butt joints (see sketch). Glue and nail a piece of ¾-inch plywood (C) to top of this frame, and a piece of ¼-inch plywood (D) to bottom.

2 Glue and screw horizontal runners (E) and end pieces (F) to outside of bed frames, keeping bottoms flush.

3 Refer to page 88 for making a dowel joint. Using five dowels between all pieces of plywood (G), assemble corner uprights. Glue all dowel joints.

4 Glue and screw beds to uprights. (The brass-plated screws are decorative—more screws are countersunk and filled.)

5 Glue and screw remaining end pieces (H) to uprights.

6 Cut squares in 1x10 ladder (I) for handholds; secure to bed.

7 Glue and screw together all drawer pieces (J, K, L, M). Attach casters to bottom.

8 Treat exposed edges of plywood with filler or veneer tape.

9 Paint or stain bed.

Materials (for project shown):

¾-in. plywood—4 shts.				
C	2	78×39 in.	**J**	1 45×8 in.
G	12	18×20 in.	**K**	2 24×8 in.
F,H	6	40½×9 in.	**E**	4 78×9 in.
L	1	43½×8 in.		

½-in. plywood—¼ sht.		
M	1	44×23½ in.

¼-in. plywood—2 shts.		
D	2	78×39 in.

1×10 pine—4 ft.		
I	1	48 in.

2×4 pine—56 ft.				
A	4	78 in.	**B**	8 36 in.

¼-in. dowels—27 ft.		
	40	8 in.

Casters, glue, paint or stain, and wood filler or veneer tape.

WOOD-BLOCK HEADBOARD

If you're the type of wood-worker who hates to throw away scrap pieces of lumber, this is your project. A random pattern of various sizes, types, and thicknesses of wood provides visual impact, and a piece of plywood backing holds the whole thing together securely.

1 Rabbet the back edges of 2x4s (A, B) ½ inch to accommodate the plywood backing (C).
2 Miter ends of 2x4s. Glue; nail together. Nail plywood to frame.
3 Paint frame and plywood, as shown, or finish as desired.
4 Lay out blocks on the floor in an interesting pattern; transfer to plywood and glue in place.
5 Position headboard.

Materials (for project shown):

¹/₂-in. plywood—1 sht.
  C 1 52×46 in.
2×4—18 ft.
  A 2 48 in.   **B** 2 54 in.
Wood blocks, paint, and finish.

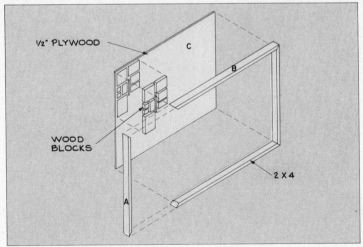

½" PLYWOOD

C

B

WOOD BLOCKS

2 X 4

A

DRESSED-UP HEADBOARD

This bed unit combines a sturdy frame and versatile shelving in a minimum of floor space. Headboard detail comes from 1x3 flooring placed at a 45-degree angle, but horizontal, vertical, or chevron patterns are other possibilities. If space is limited, build just the bed frame.

1 For bed frame, lay long 2x6s (A) and spacers (B, C) on edge. Glue and nail together.
2 Top base with plywood (D); secure 1x8s (E, F) around edge.
3 Using 2x6s for horizontals (G) and uprights (H), glue and nail center panel frame together.
4 Fasten plywood (I), 1x3 flooring (J), and 1x8 (K) to frame.
5 For side units, dado inside of cabinet sides (L) for shelf hardware, and cut ½-inch-wide rabbets in back edges for backing (M). Notch sides for toe space. Assemble top (N) and sides with mitered corners; nail bottom shelf (O) and backing in place.
6 Install hardware, shelves (P).
7 Screw units together; glue and nail 1x6 base (Q) to front.
8 Fill edges of plywood.
9 Sand; finish as desired.

Materials (for project shown):

2x6 pine or fir—60 ft.

A	4	80 in.	**G**	2	63 in.
B	2	26 in.	**H**	4	26¼ in.
C	4	6 in.			

1×8 pine or fir—32 ft.

E	2	81½ in.	**K**	1	63 in.
F	2	56 in.			

1×6 pine or fir—8 ft.

Q 1 90 in.

¾-in. plywood—2½ shts.

D	2	40×56 in.	**O**	2	9¾×12 in.
L	4	10×42 in.			
N	2	10×13½ in.			
P	4	9¾×11¾ in.			

½-in. plywood—½ sht.

I 1 29¼×63 in.

¼-in. plywood—½ sht.

M 2 13×41¾ in.

1×3 flooring (J)—70 ft.

Shelf hardware, glue, and wood filler or veneer tape.

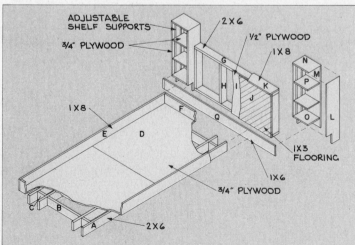

ADJUSTABLE SHELF SUPPORTS
¾" PLYWOOD
2 X 6
½" PLYWOOD
1X8
1X8
G
H I J K
N
M
P
O L
E D
F Q
1X6
¾" PLYWOOD
C B A
2 X 6
1X3 FLOORING

HEADS-UP LOUNGE

As a spot for reading, relaxing, or good conversation, this stylish lounge is tops. Build the sturdy frame from 1x12s and 2x12s, then top it with an upholstered mattress. To complete the down-low look, build the matching table, which is just a simple box.

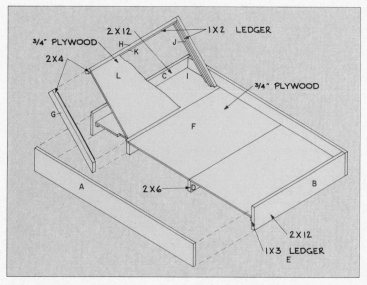

1 Cut pieces for frame (A, B, C); assemble with butt joints.

2 Position 2x6s (D) on edge as stretchers between sides of frame to support plywood bottom pieces. Screw to 2x12s.

3 Glue and screw 1x3 ledgers (E) to ends of bed frame.

4 Glue and nail two 40-inch plywood pieces (F) to frame.

5 Angle-cut 2x4 headboard frame side pieces (G) at 45 degrees (see sketch). Screw angled end of sides to 2x6 and 2x12s of bed frame. Screw 2x4 headboard frame end piece (H) to side pieces.

6 Notch plywood (I) around 2x4s. Glue and nail to frame.

7 Angle-cut 1x2 ledgers (J) at 45 degrees; fasten all ledgers (J, K) to headboard frame.

8 Bevel plywood headboard (L) at 45 degrees. And glue and nail to headboard frame.

9 Sand, finish unit.

10 Upholster mattress and cushion (see page 95).

Materials (for project shown):

2×12—26 ft.
| **A** | 2 | 96 in. | **B** | 1 | 55 in. |
| **C** | 1 | 58 in. | | | |

2×6—10 ft.
| **D** | 2 | 55 in. | | | |

1×3—10 ft.
| **E** | 2 | 55 in. | | | |

2×4—10 ft.
| **G** | 2 | 29 in. | | | |
| **H** | 1 | 52 in. | | | |

1×2—10 ft.
| **J** | 2 | 20¼ in. | **K** | 1 | 52 in. |

¾-in. plywood—2 shts.
| **F** | 2 | 55×40 in. | **L** | 1 | 52×21 in. |
| **I** | 1 | 55×14½ in. | | | |

Double mattress, foam cushion for headboard, upholstery fabric, glue, stain, and varnish.

FANCY FOLDAWAY BED

Foldaway beds have been around for a long time, but this updated version has a couple of new twists. The swing-out storage bins not only support the weight of the bed, they're also handy catchalls. And the shelving unit above the bed is the perfect stash for everything from books to bongos.

1 This project is designed to accommodate a 39x75-inch mattress. But you can easily adjust measurements to fit the size you'll use.

2 For bed frame, position 1x4s (A, B) on edge. Glue and nail together. Glue and nail to plywood bottom (C).

3 For surround, build top (D) and sides (E) of 1x10s. Glue and nail plywood backing (F, G) to frame.

4 Glue and nail vertical shelf supports (H) to end of 1x10s. Position bottom plates (I) between plywood backing and 2x2s; glue and nail in place.

5 Glue and nail 1x2 shelf ledger (J) flush with the top of vertical shelf supports. Rip shelf to 8¾ inches wide; glue and nail to vertical supports and plywood backing.

6 Secure surround to wall studs through backing; nail to floor through bottom plates.

7 Install vertical and horizontal 2x2 framing (L, M) for center panel. Position verticals (L) flush with front edge of shelf. Butt horizontal framing (M) between vertical framing and backing. Glue and nail plywood front panel (N) to framing.

8 Cut handhold from doors (O), and assemble storage bins from plywood pieces (P, Q, R) as shown. Attach casters to bins. Hinge doors to surround.

9 Install plywood bed frame stops (S) in corners of surround.

10 Assemble upper unit from 1x10s (T, U, V) and plywood (W) as shown. Screw to surround, and secure to wall.

11 Attach bed frame to shelf with piano hinge. Bed frame will be supported by vertical 2x2s on each end, plywood center support, and swing-out drawers when open (see detail).

12 Drill through shelf, top of surround, and bed frame for eyebolt "pins" (X).

13 Paint unit as desired.

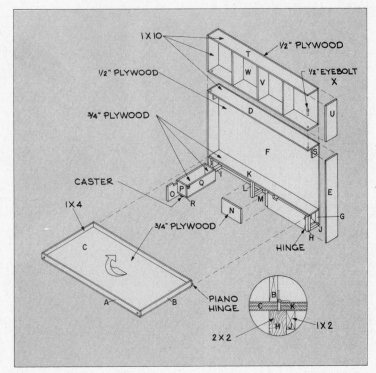

Materials (for project shown):

¾-in. plywood—1½ shts.

C	1	77½×41½ in.
S	2	5¼×5¼ in.
N	1	10½×14½ in.
O	2	30×10½ in.
P	4	8×6¼ in.
Q	2	6¼×24 in.
R	2	8¾×24 in.

½-in. plywood—2 shts.

F	1	48×79 in.
G	1	7×79 in.
W	1	24×79 in.

1×10—50 ft.

E	2	55 in.	D,K,T	4	77½ in.
V	3	22½ in.	U	2	24 in.

2×2—8 ft.

H,L	4	10½ in.	M	2	7¼ in.
I	2	8 in.			

1×4—20 ft.

A	2	77½ in.	B	2	40 in.

1×2—8 ft.

J	1	77½ in.

½-in. eyebolts (X), casters, hinges, glue, and paint.

SHIPSHAPE BUNK

The seafaring idea of supporting bunks on walls inspired this unit. A runged upright ladder adds another nautical touch.

1 For the base of each bed frame, glue and nail 2x2s (A, B) using simple butt joints (see page 86).
2 Glue and nail the ¾-inch plywood platform (C) to 2x2s.
3 Glue and nail together 1x3 trim pieces (D, E) and attach to 2x2s (see sketch).
4 Notch 2x4 crosspieces (F) to accommodate the 2x2s and 1x3s of the frame, with room on ends of 2x4s to lap uprights (G).
5 Mark one upright for dowel rungs (H) on 13-inch centers.
6 Secure crosspieces to the uprights.
7 Drill uprights for top rail (I) and ladder.
8 Glue all dowels in place.
9 Secure crosspieces to wall studs approximately 4 feet apart. (Additional 2x4 ledgers secured to the wall to support the bed frame will add stability.)
10 Secure frames in notches.
11 Sand; finish.

Materials (for project shown):

³/₄-in. plywood—2 shts.
  C 2 39×75 in.
2×4 pine or fir—24 ft.
  F 4 45 in.   **G** 2 66 in.
2×2 pine—42 ft.
  A 4 75 in.   **B** 4 36 in.
1×3 pine or fir—42 ft.
  D 4 76½ in.   **E** 4 39 in.
1¹/₄-in. dowels—10 ft.
  H 4 9½ in.   **I** 1 67 in.
Glue, and paint or stain.

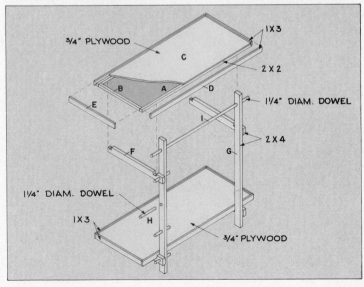

HEIRLOOM BABY CRIB

What better way to welcome a new baby to your home than with this crib? The look is a blend of old and new, with sturdy half-lap and dadoed slat sides and end panels of clear acrylic sheet. Spring bolts make the adjustable side easy to raise and lower for access to the mattress area.

1 Cut a ¼×⅜-inch-deep dado in frame members A. Glue and nail A and D to form the frame. Nail ledgers (B,C) to the inside of the frame as shown.

2 Fasten plywood (E) to frame.

3 Build side assemblies of 1x2s (F, G) and ¾×1 (H) material using half-lap and dado joints (see page 87). Space slats no farther than 3½ inches apart.

4 Install spring bolts and metal guide pins in adjustable sides.

5 Rout guide track in two legs (I) on drop-down side. Drill holes for spring bolts.

6 Cut ¾×⅜-inch rabbets in top rails (J). Dado legs for acrylic panels. Glue and nail I and J to form the leg assemblies.

7 Secure stationary side to legs using dowels (K) (see page 88). Position adjustable side between legs.

8 Sand; finish all pieces.

9 Slide acrylic panels in place, then raise the mattress platform into place; secure with screws.

Materials (for project shown):

1×4 fir—36 ft.

D	2	52 in.	**I**	4	41 in.
A	2	28¾ in.	**J**	2	30¼ in.

1×2 fir—40 ft.

B	2	27¼ in.	**F**	4	46½ in.
C	2	50½ in.	**G**	4	28 in.

¾×1 fir—44 ft.

H 22 26½ in.

½-in. plywood—1 sht.

E 1 27¼×52 in.

¼-in. acrylic sheet

L 2 29½×15½ in.

⅜-in. dowels—2 ft.

K 6 3 in.

¼-in. metal pins, spring bolts, nails, screws, glue, and finish.

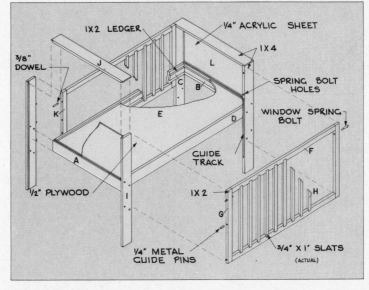

3/8" DOWEL · 1X2 LEDGER · ¼" ACRYLIC SHEET · 1X4 · SPRING BOLT HOLES · WINDOW SPRING BOLT · GUIDE TRACK · ½" PLYWOOD · 1X2 · ¼" METAL GUIDE PINS · ¾" X 1" SLATS (ACTUAL)

SENSIBLE STORAGE

Rare indeed is the household with enough storage space to suit everyone's needs. But you can end your storage crunch with style by creating one or more of the freestanding projects presented in this chapter. They're simple to build and won't cost as much as you might think.

And all of these designs are easily adapted to make units of other dimensions. Simply reposition or change the height of uprights to fit the exact space you have available. When you've completed the construction phase of your project, there's another important step—finishing the unit to fit in with your decor. Finishing is just as important as putting it together in obtaining professional results. It's often the area where the most creativity is needed. There is such a wide variety of finishes available today that you won't have any trouble at all finding exactly what you need to crown your storage project with the finishing touch.

NO-NAILS STORAGE CUBES

This eye-catching storage unit gets its inspiration from a house of cards, and is almost as easy to build. The simplicity of the design allows you to assemble the unit in any number of ways. And, since there's no connecting hardware, it's all perfectly portable.

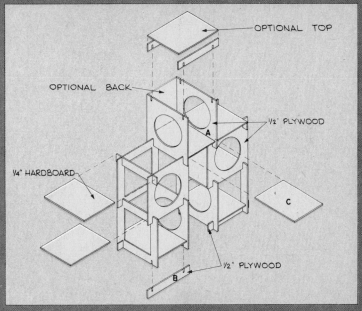

1 In each top and bottom edge of ten ½-inch plywood squares (A), cut two 2-inch-deep, ½-inch-wide notches. Position the outside edge of these notches 3 inches from the edges of the plywood pieces as shown.

2 Similarly, notch all eight horizontal braces (B) on one edge. Sand each piece smooth.

3 On six of the squares, center 18-inch-diameter circles. (Tie a length of string to a pencil or scribe. Mark off 9 inches of the string and tack to square's center at this point. Swing an arc to form circle.) On the four remaining squares, center 18-inch squares. Cut out inside shapes and sand edges smooth.

4 Following manufacturer's directions, apply veneer or wood tape to exposed inside and outside edges of plywood. Or, use wood putty and sand smooth.

5 Stain or paint both sides of plywood. Treat edges to match, or paint a contrasting color.

6 Paint hardboard shelves (C) as desired. Hardboard for top and back of highest cube is optional. (For a lighter look, substitute clear or tinted acrylic sheet for hardboard.)

7 Assemble unit as shown.

Materials (for project shown):

½-inch plywood—2 shts.
  A 10 24×24 in.   B 8 24×4 in.
¼-inch hardboard—1 or 1¼ shts.
  C 7 or 9. 24×18 in.
Wood tape or veneer—approx. 250 ft.
Paint or stain.

TALL BOY
CHINA
CABINET

1 Construct the cabinet frame (A,B), using ¾-inch plywood. Nail the top, bottom, and shelf (C) into place. Position top piece C three inches down from top of frame (A,B).
2 Attach 1x2s (D) and 1x1 (E).
3 For base, miter and nail 2x4s (F, G) together; center and nail plywood subbase (H) to 2x4s, and secure to cabinet bottom.
4 To trim, nail 1x3s (I, J) around edge; center and nail plywood top (K). Refer to detail and apply cove molding (L, M), window stop (N, O), and half-round (P, Q) as shown.
5 Install shelving (R) and shutters (S). (Refer to page 93 for hanging a door.)
6 Install catches and pull rings.
7 Paint or stain cabinet.

Materials (for project shown):

¾-inch plywood—2 shts.
  A 2 16×75 in. **B** 1 18½×75 in.
  C 3 18½×15¼ in.
  R 6 18¼×15 in.
H,K 2 21½×17½ in.
2×4—8 ft.
  F 2 21½ in.   **G** 2 17½ in.
1×2—14 ft.
  D 2 75 in.
1×1—2 ft.
  E 1 17 in.
1×3—8 ft.
  I 2 21½ in.   **J** 2 16 in.
¾×¾-in. cove molding—10 ft.
  L 2 21½ in.   **M** 4 17½ in.
Colonial door stop—6 ft.
  N 1 22½ in.   **O** 2 18 in.
Half-round—6 ft.
  P 1 23¼ in.   **Q** 2 18⅜ in.
Blank shutters
  S 4 approximately 9×36 in.
Adjustable shelf hardware, magnetic catch hardware, pull rings, and paint or stain.

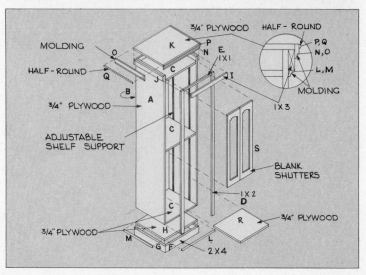

CUSTOM ENTERTAINMENT CENTER

This unit almost plans itself. The dimensions of your television, stereo equipment, and books determine the inside shelf dimensions. With almost 30 feet of shelf space, this unit is a natural focal point for your living or family room—and the mahogany plywood has all the warmth of the finest furniture.

1 Determine position of all shelves, and dado uprights (A) ¼ inch to receive them.
2 Build box of dadoed uprights and horizontals (B), mitering four outside corners. Screw plywood subbase (C) to bottom, flush to rear.
3 If desired, dado shelves (D) for small vertical divider (E).
4 Glue shelves (D, F) into dadoes and strengthen with permanent shelf brackets where necessary.
5 Apply 1¼-inch mahogany trim (G, H, I) to front edges of uprights and shelves. Butt-join all pieces together, and apply vertical pieces of trim to outside box first, then uprights. Top of trim is flush with top of horizontals. Vertical trim lies flush with outside of outer uprights, and is centered on the middle uprights.
6 Sand; stain and varnish.
7 Nail prefinished mahogany paneling to back of unit.

Materials (for project shown):
¾-inch mahogany plywood—3 shts.

A	4 66×16 in.	**C**	1	62×15 in.
F	1 16×6 in.	**D**	6	16×18½ in.
B	2 16×64¾ in.	**E**	4	16×27½ in.

G,H,I 1¼-in. mahogany trim—52 ft.
J Mahogany paneling—2 shts.
Glue, stain to match paneling, varnish, shelf brackets.

LATTICEWORK PLANT SHELTER

House your favorite light-seeking plants in this turn-of-the-century style structure. Its airy, gazebo charm comes from diagonal latticework and a pristine coat of white paint. If you can't locate the unit near a window, install fluorescent lighting to keep your greenery healthy and happy.

1 Cut center openings in plywood ends (A) as shown in sketch.

2 To assemble bottom of unit, glue and nail sides (B) to bottom piece (C) with butt joints.

3 Secure ends to lower box.

4 Cut top plywood front pieces (D) as shown (or in pattern desired). Glue and nail to uprights.

5 Space 1x4 crosspieces (E) on edge equally between uprights. Glue and nail in place.

6 Cap edges of uprights with veneer strips (F). Trim tops and bottoms of lower box with horizontal veneer strips (G).

7 On sides, nail lattice strips (H) at 45-degree angle to inside of uprights. (Use one piece as a cutting guide for the rest.)

8 To duplicate chevron pattern on front, divide panel equally with a vertical line. Begin applying lattice strips (H) at 45-degree angle from bottom of this line in both directions. Fill corners with shorter pieces, and butt center pieces together along line to form V-shape.

9 Nail lattice trim (I) beneath lattice strips.

10 Sand and paint unit.

Materials (for project shown):

1-in. plywood—1½ shts.
  A 2 18×78 in. **B** 2 46×15 in.
  C 1 46×16 in. **D** 2 46×9 in.
1×4—10 ft.
  E 7 16 in.
1×¼-in. veneer strips—32 ft.
  F 4 78 in.
¼×1½-in. lattice strips—140 ft.
  I 2 18 in.   **G** 4 45½ in.
  H 120 ft. for trim
Glue and paint.

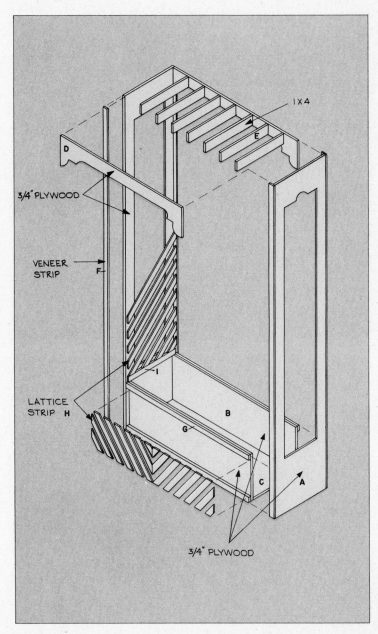

1X4

E

D

3/4" PLYWOOD

VENEER STRIP

F

I

LATTICE STRIP H

G

B

C

A

3/4" PLYWOOD

MODULAR STORAGE/WORK CENTER

Modular furniture is perfect for today's on-the-go families who need flexible, durable storage and work space. This unit, with its simple design and solid construction, makes great furniture for any room in the house. And, the units are completely re-stackable for quick-change decorating.

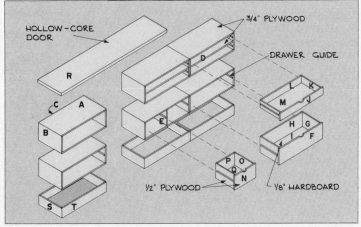

HOLLOW-CORE DOOR
3/4" PLYWOOD
DRAWER GUIDE
1/2" PLYWOOD
1/8" HARDBOARD

1 From ¾-inch plywood (A, B, C), build six boxes for shells of unit. Place horizontal (D) and vertical (E) plywood dividers for shallow and narrow drawers. Fasten side-mounted drawer guides to uprights inside cabinet shells where drawers are desired.

2 For drawers, cut ½-inch plywood and hardboard (F through Q) to size. Cut 3-inch-diameter semicircular handholds from top of drawer fronts. Make ¼-inch-wide, ¼-inch-deep dadoes in drawer members to receive bottoms. Assemble sides of drawers with simple butt joints. Fit and nail hardboard bottoms into position.

3 Build three 6-inch-high bases of ¾-inch plywood (S, T).

4 For desk top, use an 18-inch-wide hollow core door (R) or double thicknesses of ¾-inch plywood screwed together.

5 Paint unit and stack in desired position. Position desk top.

6 Position drawers in place.

Materials (for project shown):

¾-inch plywood—4½ shts.
- **A** 12 36×18 in.
- **B** 12 12×18 in.
- **C** 6 12×34½ in.
- **E** 1 12×17¼ in.
- **D** 2 34½×17¼ in.
- **T** 6 36×6 in.
- **S** 6 16½×6 in.

½-in. plywood—1½ shts.
For two wide, deep drawers:
- **F** 2 34⅜×11⅞ in.
- **G** 4 16×11¾ in.
- **H** 2 32½×11¾ in.

For four wide, shallow drawers:
- **J** 4 34⅜×5½ in.
- **K** 8 16×5⅜ in.
- **L** 4 32½×5⅜ in.

For two narrow, deep drawers:
- **N** 2 16¾×11⅞ in.
- **O** 4 16×11¾ in.
- **P** 2 14⅞×11¾ in.

⅛-in. hardboard—1½ shts.
- **I** 2 33×16 in.
- **M** 4 33×16 in.
- **Q** 2 15⅜×16 in.

18-inch hollow core door (R), glue, side-mounted drawer guides, and paint.

INSTANT DOWEL BOOKCASE

This simple project transforms dowels and 1x12s into a something different bookcase. Though it takes only a few hours to construct, it's one of the best ways going to get sturdy shelf space.

1 Locate top shelf position on 1x12 upright (A) by measuring down 6 inches from one end. Square a horizontal line across at this point. Similarly, mark horizontal position of other two shelves at 10-inch intervals below this shelf.

2 On horizontal line, mark centers of two outer dowels 2 inches from edges of 1x12. Mark the centers of the two inner shelf dowels equidistant from these two marks.

3 Mark dowel locations for other two shelves similarly.

4 Locate book support dowel 3 inches above rear shelf dowel and 2 inches from edge of 1x12.

5 Clamp the three 1x12s together with C-clamps (place a lumber scrap between clamps and 1x12s to avoid marring the wood). Drill through all three thicknesses at center mark of each dowel location with a ¾-inch bit.

6 Insert dowels (B) through 1x12s using a rubber mallet, if needed; glue dowels in position.

7 Sand, and paint or stain.

Materials (for project shown):
¾-in. dowels—46 ft.
  B 15 36 in.
1×12—8 ft.
  A 3 30 in.
Glue, and paint or stain.

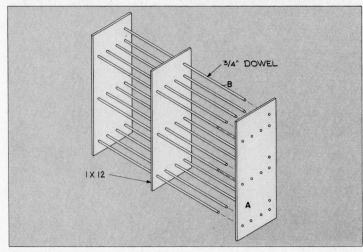

PLANT-LOVING BOOKSHELF

If your would-be plant room is cramped for shelf space and low on light exposure, this unit was made for you. Adjustable shelves make for flexible storage, and the lighted top shelf will pamper even the most finicky houseplants. Install a fixture on a lower shelf for still more greenery.

1 Dado 1x10 uprights (A) for shelf hardware. Butt-join and nail top (B) between uprights. Nail 1x2 (C) on edge between uprights, position bottom shelf (D), and nail in place.
2 Glue and nail plywood (E) to back of shelf.
3 Secure adjustable shelving hardware (F) to uprights.
4 Attach a two-tube fluorescent light fixture to the underside of the top shelf. Drill a hole through back of bookcase for electrical cord. (It would be a good idea to install a switched electrical cord in light fixture.)
5 Nail 1x4 (G) on edge.
6 Install shelving hardware and shelves (H).
7 Paint or stain unit, if desired.

Materials (for project shown):
½-in. plywood—1 sht.
    E 1 48×72 in.
1×10—36 ft.
    A 2 72 in.   **H** 4 46¼ in.
  B,D 2 46½ in.
1×2—4 ft.
    C 1 46½ in.
1×4—4 ft.
    G 1 46½ in.
Adjustable shelving hardware (F), fluorescent light fixture, and switched electrical cord.

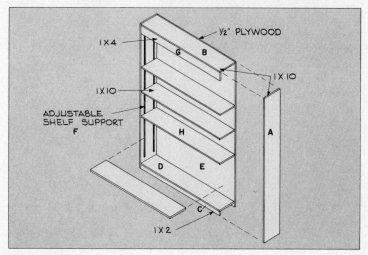

FOR CHILDREN ONLY

If kids could build their own furniture, they'd make something colorful and comfortable and free of tough-to-tangle-with hardware. Parents might design much the same thing, but with a bit of practicality and durability thrown in, too.

The six children's projects presented in this section fill that bill admirably, and all are pieces kids will love to have in their rooms. They'll delight in using things you've made especially for them ... and you'll have the satisfaction of giving them something of lasting value.

Good kids' furniture is scarce—and usually expensive. But not the projects we've selected. All are low-cost alternatives to higher priced ready-mades. And they're at least as sturdy as their store-bought counterparts.

And one more thing ... building one of these projects just might make you feel like a kid again, too.

CIRCUS WAGON TOY CHEST

That great childhood dread—room cleaning—becomes a snap when your kids use this colorful toy chest. Painted brightly in carnival colors, it looks exactly like a circus wagon—and it works just as hard, too. Cage yours with a not-so-ferocious feline such as this one, or your own favorite beast.

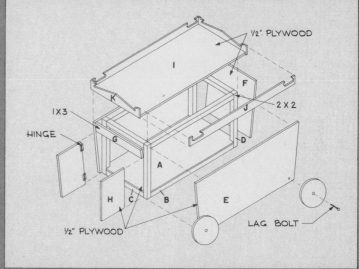

1 For frame, notch plywood bottom (A) in all corners. Glue and nail bottom 2x2s (B, C) to plywood. Glue and nail 2x2 uprights (D) and top pieces (B, C) together for remainder of frame. Secure to bottom assembly.
2 For trapezoidal sides (E), make a mark 3 inches in from both ends along bottom of plywood; cut along these lines to form trapezoid. (To simplify the project, eliminate this step and cut plywood side pieces 36 inches wide. Adjust size of plywood back and doors to fit.)
3 Glue and nail sides to frame. Position back piece (F) between sides; glue and nail in place.
4 Position 1x3 door header (G) between sides at top front; glue and nail.
5 Hang doors (H) beneath 1x3 (you may want to install magnet-ic catch hardware to inside of frame to keep doors closed).
5 Nail plywood top (I) to frame. Using a saber saw or coping saw, cut scrollwork from plywood (J, K) for trim. Glue and nail these pieces together and nail trim assembly to top.
7 Attach wheels (L) to frame.
8 Sand; paint.

Materials (for project shown):
2×2—24 ft.
B	4 33 in.	**C**	4 15 in.
D	4 18 in.		

½-in. plywood—1 sht.
A	1 18×36 in.	**H**	2 15½×9 in.
E	2 18×42 in.	**J**	2 4×43 in.
F	1 18×18 in.	**K**	2 4×20 in.
I	1 19×43 in.	**L**	4 9-in. diam.

1×3—2 ft.
G 1 18 in.
Lag bolts, washers, hinges, and paint.

DECKED-OUT CHAIR

Although its simple lines and redwood construction suggest patio furniture, this chair is designed for the great indoors. But it still has all the sturdiness of outdoor furniture, which makes it ideal for kids of all ages. Strap a rolled, fabric-filled piece of foam to the back for extra comfort.

1 Standing the frame's front (A) and sides (B) on edge, glue and screw the pieces together using butt-joints (see page 86). If desired, brace corners on the inside of frame with angle brackets for additional strength.

2 Position the lower back brace (C) between seat frame sides at angle shown in the detail accompanying the sketch. Glue and screw in place.

3 Glue and screw upper back brace (D) to rear pair of legs (E).

4 Position rear leg assembly and front legs so that top of seat is 10 to 12 inches from the floor (cushion will add extra height); glue and screw in place.

5 Glue and nail the six back pieces (F) to supports.

6 Glue and nail nine seat pieces (G) to seat frame.

7 Glue and screw armrests (H) to tops of legs.

8 Sand; paint or stain.

9 Trim foam seat cushion to fit, if necessary, and cover with upholstery fabric (see page 95).

10 Cover back cushion similarly; roll up and strap to back with webbing.

Materials (for project shown):

5/4×3 redwood—24 ft.

A	1	17⅞ in.
B	2	22 in.
C	1	17⅞ in.
D	1	20 in.
E	4	19 in.
H	2	24⅛ in.

5/4×2 redwood—30 ft.

G 9 20 in. **F** 6 12½ in.

Foam for cushions, upholstery fabric to cover cushions, length of webbing, glue, and paint or stain.

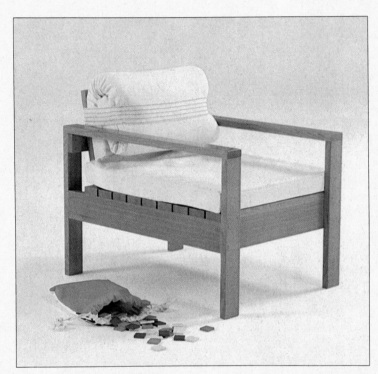

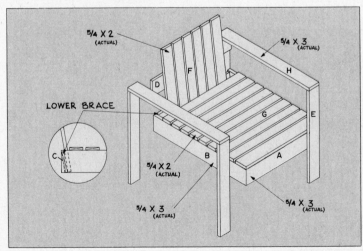

LOWER BRACE

5/4 X 2 (ACTUAL)

5/4 X 3 (ACTUAL)

5/4 X 2 (ACTUAL)

5/4 X 3 (ACTUAL)

5/4 X 3 (ACTUAL)

BROWN COW STORAGE CHEST

Your little tenderfoot won't get saddle sore from this friendly critter. And he'll have just as much fun playing with this chest as with the toys and games it holds. For a finishing touch, fashion a jaunty tail from a frayed rope.

1 Cut off both bottom corners of the three 12x11½ inch pieces of plywood (A) at a 45-degree angle so that cut edge measures 3½ inches.

2 Cut top corners from the two 12x4¾-inch pieces (B) similarly.

3 To construct the cow's body, glue and screw the plywood members (C,D) to the end members (A) as shown in the sketch. Position the divider as shown, then glue and screw it to the sides.

4 Cut a 1½x5-inch handhold from one of the lid's members, using a saber saw. (Be sure to smooth the corners.)

5 Round off tops of legs (E), and taper bottom to 4 inches.

6 Angle-cut bottoms of legs to rest flat on the floor.

7 Glue and screw all four legs to body.

8 Cut cow's head shape (F) from plywood (for safety's sake, remember to keep shape free of dangerous edges).

9 Notch cow's head adjacent to lid ¼ inch for clearance.

10 Drill holes in head for eye and handhold dowel (G). Glue dowel in place. Center head on body; glue and screw in place.

11 Drill hole for tail. Knot rope inside box; fray edges for tail.

12 Attach lid to body with hinge.

Materials (for project shown):

¾-in. plywood—1 sht.

A	3	12×11½ in.	**D**	8	3½×30 in.
B	2	12×4¾ in.	**E**	4	5×18½ in.
C	10	2¼×30 in.	**F**	1	15¼×13 in.

¾-in. dowel—1 ft.

G 1 8 in.

Length of rope and piano hinge.

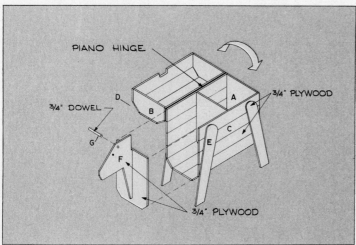

PIANO HINGE

¾" DOWEL

D

B

A

¾" PLYWOOD

G

E

C

F

¾" PLYWOOD

KID-SIZED TABLE AND CHAIRS

Be prepared to host a host of get-togethers when you build your kids this scaled-down table and chairs set. The miniature table is custom-designed to make the best use of materials, and the unusual chairs are assembled from six carefully shaped pieces of plywood.

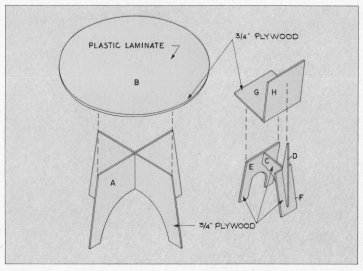

1 For table base, make a mark on top edges of plywood rectangles (A) 2 inches in from upper corners. Draw a line from this mark to lower corners. Cut along these lines to form trapezoids.
2 Cut arc from bottoms of these pieces (see sketch).
3 To assemble, mark horizontal center, and extend line vertically between top of plywood and top of arc. Mark center of this vertical line. Cut a ¾-inch-wide notch down to center point from top of one piece, and up to center point from top of arc on other piece.
4 Glue and interlock base pieces together.
5 Cut plywood circle (B) for tabletop. Apply plastic laminate to top and 1½-inch strip to outside edge. (If desired, omit plastic laminate, and apply wood tape or filler to exposed edges of ply-wood, then paint.) Glue and nail tabletop to base.
6 For chairs, cut 7-inch-radius curve from seat braces (C) as shown. Cut braces for rear support (D) as shown. (As an option, you could cut these braces as one T-shaped piece, and notch to the rear support (F).)
7 Cut arc in front supports (E).
8 Glue and screw front and rear supports to braces.
9 Round front edge of seats (G). Glue and screw seats and backs (H) to braces and supports.
10 Sand and paint.

Materials (for project shown):

¾-in. plywood—1½ shts.

B	1	32-in. diam.	**E**	4	12×12 in.
A	2	24×21¼ in.	**F**	4	6×11 in.
C	4	8×9 in.	**G**	4	12×12 in.
D	4	3×18 in.	**H**	4	12×13¼ in.

Glue, paint, plastic laminate, and adhesive.

HIGH-STYLE HIGH CHAIR

1 Lay 1-inch dowels (A) on the floor in a trapezoid formation. Cut tops and bottoms level.

2 Drill beveled 1x2 seat supports (B) to accommodate legs.

3 Round outside corners, and glue and screw 1x2 base assembly (C, D) together. Secure dowels to base using lap joints (see page 86).

4 Round out half-circles in footrest (E) and screw to legs.

5 For top assembly, angle-cut one end of 1x2 armrests (F). Round off corners of plywood seat (G). Drill holes in seat and 1x2s (F, H) for 14 ½-inch dowels (I). Glue dowels in place.

6 Cut rectangle from plywood tray (J), rounding corners (see sketch). Angle-cut one end of tray supports (K), and cut semi-circular notches from other ends.

7 Drill 1-inch holes in armrests to accommodate tray support dowels (L). Glue dowels.

8 Screw hardwood locking tabs to tray supports and attach tray.

9 Screw top assembly to base.

10 Finish as desired.

Materials (for project shown):

1-in. wood dowels—12 ft.
    A 4 24 in.   **L** 2 1¾ in.
½-in. wood dowels—12 ft.
    I 14 8½ in.
1×2 hardwood—12 ft.
    B,C 2 16 in.   **F,K** 4 15 in.
    D,H 2 13½ in.
¾-in. plywood—¼ sht.
    G 1 15×16 in.
    J 1 10×14 in.
1×3 hardwood—2 ft.
    E 1 15 in.
Small pieces of hardwood for locking tabs, glue, and paint or stain.

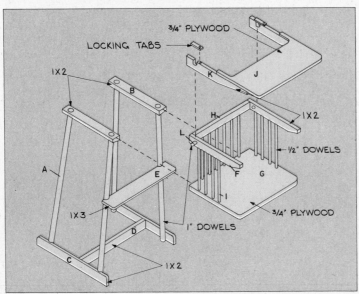

SUPER-SIMPLE STORAGE AND SEATING

Besides being a colorful play table, this easy-do unit is a clever catchall for a multitude of treasures. And, the mini-cubes tuck underneath when not being used. Enamel with bright paint-box colors for a finishing touch.

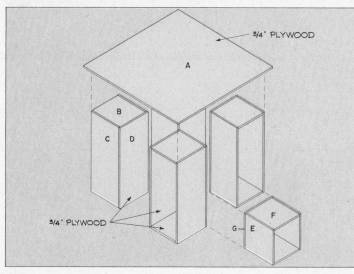

1 Construct seating cubes and table bases as shown in sketch. Assemble with glue and screws.
2 Cover the exposed plywood edges with wood tape or use filler, and finish as desired.
3 Screw top to base.

Materials (for project shown):

³/₄-in. plywood—2¹/₂ shts.
For table:

A	1	39×39 in.
B	8	10½×11¼ in.
C	8	11¼×24 in.
D	4	12×24 in.

For seating cubes:

E	8	12×11¼ in.
F	8	10½×11¼ in.
G	4	12×12 in.

Wood tape or filler, glue, paint.

OUTDOOR PROJECTS

Looking for fine wood furniture that's safe to leave outside on your porch, deck, or patio? If so, look no further—here are some great ideas! The projects in this chapter are designed to stand up beautifully to sun, rain, and the rigors of seasonal temperature changes.

Yet, despite their extra-rugged character, they're also the kind of graceful, good-looking furniture ideas you'll be proud to use day after day.

As a bonus, you'll find that these outdoor projects add living space to your home by providing an inviting oasis for friendly conversations, entertaining, or just plain relaxing.

So plan to build one soon. Choose a backyard bench or table . . . a beautiful porch swing . . . or even a canopied glider. They're all waiting to add a little freedom to your life style. You'll admire and enjoy the rewards of your creative craftsmanship for years to come!

TRADITIONAL PORCH SWING

Forget the tensions of a busy day by settling into this comfortable, laid-back porch swing. It's easy to build from redwood lumber sanded smooth and sealed with several coats of exterior varnish. For added comfort, make weatherproof seat cushions from canvas or vinyl-covered foam padding (see instructions for making cushions on page 95).

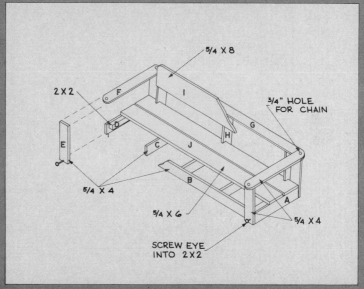

1 Construct framework for seat by butting together 5/4x4 lumber (A, B) and strengthening with 5/4x4 and 2x2 crosspieces (C, D). Use glue and screws at all joints, countersinking screwheads and filling holes.

2 Glue and screw vertical armrest supports (E) to the frame. Lap-joint armrests (F) and top rail (G). Then drill holes in the armrests and round corners as shown; glue and screw to supports.

3 Cut notches in vertical seat back supports (H). You can adjust the angle of your seat back by tapering the supports. Glue and screw to seat frame.

4 Round corners of a 5/4x8 for seat back (I). Also cut lengths of 5/4x6 to form seat (J). Wait to install.

5 Seal, stain (if desired), and varnish all pieces.

6 When dry, attach back (I) and evenly spaced seat planks (J) to frame. Install eyebolts and chain (strong enough to support 400 pounds).

Materials (for a 60×25-inch swing):

5/4×8 redwood—6 ft.
  I 1 51 in.
5/4×6 redwood—16 ft.
  J 3 60 in.
5/4×4 redwood—42 ft.

A	2	19 in.	**F**	2	25 in.
C	3	16¾ in.	**E,H**	7	14½ in.
G	1	60 in.			
B	2	57¾ in.			

2×2 redwood—4 ft.
  D   16¾ in.
Eyebolts, chain, glue, screws, sealer, stain (optional), and varnish.

LATTICE-TOP PATIO TABLE

Those odd pieces of scrap lumber cluttering your basement and garage are the perfect no-cost materials for this patio table. If you're short some necessary boards, pick them up for a few cents at the lumberyard and you're in business! Redwood works best and weathers well even without treatment. With other woods, apply varnish.

NOTE: You can achieve the rough-hewn, hand-carved effect shown by shaving the table legs and top frame members with a draw-knife before you assemble the unit.

1 Build a frame for the tabletop from 2x3 lumber cut to size (A, B). Nail together using butt joints, countersinking nailheads and filling holes, if desired.

2 Crisscross strips of lath (C) to form the double-layered tabletop surface. Miter ends of strips as necessary. Glue overlapping strips together; also glue and nail lath to tabletop frame.

3 Cut notches in pieces of 1x2 lumber (D) for crosslap joints on legs (see sketch). Miter one end of each 1x2 so legs will stand up evenly. Join pieces to form table leg assemblies as shown, gluing and screwing together. Glue and screw one set of legs to each end of tabletop.

4 Strengthen legs with evenly spaced lath strips (E) as shown in sketch. Glue and nail each strip into position.

5 Stain and varnish table, or leave unfinished to weather naturally.

Materials (for a 30×18-inch table):

2×3 redwood, pine, or fir—8 ft.
  A 2 18 in.
  B 2 27 in.
1×2 redwood, pine, or fir—10 ft.
  D 4 26 in.
Lath strips—58 ft.
  C   35 feet for tabletop
  E 8 31½ in.
Galvanized nails, screws, glue, stain (optional), and varnish (optional).

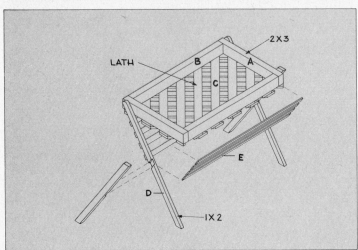

ROPE-STRUNG LAWN BENCHES

1" DOWEL

D

C

1X3 OAK

B

A

WOOD PLUG OVER SCREWS

HOLE FOR ROPE

If you need some sharp-looking seating for backyard get-togethers, you'll want to build several of these clever, portable sit-upons. The seats are soft and comfortable because they're formed from nylon rope wound and re-wound around dowels. Hardwood legs make these benches practical and beautiful.

1 Cut 1x3 legs (A), rounding off tops as shown. Drill a 1-inch hole in each leg; also notch each leg to accommodate horizontal crosspieces (see sketch).

2 Glue and screw crosspieces (B) into notches on legs. Countersink screwheads, filling holes with wood plugs. Drill a single ½-inch hole in each crosspiece for tying down rope ends.

3 Butt stretchers (C) against crosspieces, attaching with glue and screws. Again, cover screwheads with plugs.

4 Install 1-inch dowels (D) by gluing into previously drilled holes in table legs.

5 Stain and varnish bench.

6 When bench is dry, fashion rope seat. Tie down one end of rope to hole in crosspiece (B), and wind rope in a "figure 8" around dowels. Wind tightly for a firm seat; tie down loose end in opposite crosspiece.

Materials (for one bench):

1×3 oak or maple—14 ft.
 A,C 6 19 in. **B** 2 18 in.
1-inch dowel—3 ft.
 D 2 18 in.
50 feet nylon rope, wood plugs, screws, glue, stain, and varnish.

CANOPIED GLIDER

Close your eyes . . . forget the day's problems . . . and imagine you're taking an effortless, rhythmic swing aboard this whisper-quiet glider. The lattice canopy lets you enjoy blue sky and filtered sunlight while you chat with a friend. But even before you use it, you'll have the personal satisfaction of having built this backyard beauty yourself.

1 First, build two bench assemblies. Butt 1x3s and 1x2s (A, B) to form frame for seat. Nail on evenly spaced slats (C).

2 Build each armrest/side panel for seats from a plywood panel (D) and framing pieces (E, F). Taper vertical pieces (F) as shown in the sketch.

3 Construct seat back assembly from 1x4 slats (G) spaced evenly and nailed to 1x3 verticals (H) as shown. Taper verticals to fit flush against frame of seat.

4 Assemble benches by screwing seat, seat back, and armrests together. Include a 1x3 spacer (I) between armrests and seat back (see sketch).

5 Construct footrest from evenly spaced slats (J) nailed to crosspieces (K). Use a double thickness of 1x3 crosspieces on each end of footrest for strength.

6 Next, construct the canopy top and support legs. Build the top from 2x4 rails (L) and crosspieces (M), butted together with screws and glue. Countersink screwheads and fill holes. NOTE: Locate crosspieces (M) carefully. They must be proper distance apart to support benches and foot platform.

7 Nail 1x3 boards (N) onto top frame, spacing for lattice-type effect. Follow with a brace (O) down the center of the top.

8 Cut four long lengths of 2x4 to form support legs (P). Miter each end of 2x4s as shown. Working with canopy upside down on ground, bolt each leg to the top using two bolts per leg.

9 Use large wood screws inserted through pre-drilled holes to attach a bent steel strap (Q) between the two legs on each side of top (see sketch).

10 Stand canopy upright. Screw a crossbrace (R) between both sets of legs as shown.

11 Locate steel angle bars (S) in proper position on 2x4 canopy crosspieces. Screw into place.

12 Attach galvanized pipes (T, U) to angle bars (see sketch detail). Then, hang the two bench assemblies and the foot platform from the lengths of pipe as shown. Insert bolts through pre-drilled holes, using washers on each side of pipe.

13 Paint or stain and varnish.

Materials (for glider shown):

³/₄-inch plywood—1 sht.

E 4 3½×25½ in.

D 4 18×22½ in.

2×4 pine—76 ft.

P 4 9 ft.   **L** 2 96 in.

M 4 57 in.

F 8 17¼ in.

2×2 pine—10 ft.

O 1 9 ft.

1×6 pine—12 ft.

R 2 63 in.

1×4 pine—104 ft.

J,C 18 44 in.   **G** 8 42½ in.

1×3 pine—192 ft.

K 4 34 in.   **A** 4 42½ in.

H 4 20 in.   **I** 4 2½ in.

N 31 60 in.

1×2 pine—8 ft.

B 4 25½ in.

1-inch galvanized pipe (**T,U**), two pre-bent steel straps (**Q**), nuts, bolts, washers, eight angle bars (**S**), screws, nails, wood filler, paint or stain, and varnish.

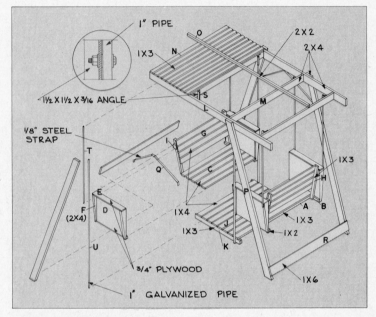

1" PIPE — 1X3 — N — O — 2 X 2 — 2 X 4 — 1½ X 1½ X 3/16 ANGLE — ⅛" STEEL STRAP — S — M — L — T — I — G — 1X3 — A — H — Q — C — B — E — F (2X4) — D — P — 1X4 — J — A B — 1X3 — 1X3 — 1X2 — U — K — R — 3/4" PLYWOOD — 1X6 — 1" GALVANIZED PIPE

CONVERTIBLE PATIO BENCH

Few do-it-yourself home projects work harder than this one. You'll have lots of roomy seating when you build a pair of these rugged benches for your patio. Then, at your next outdoor get-together, amaze your friends with your ingenuity by facing the benches toward each other and rotating their backs to create a standard-size picnic table.

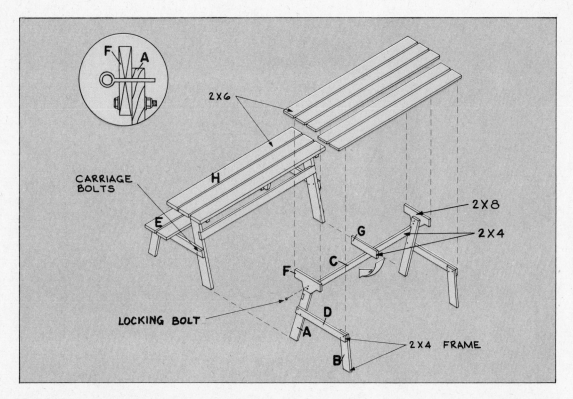

1 Start by building the 2x4 frame. Cut four sections of 2x4 to form legs (A, B). Miter ends of each leg as shown.
2 Make 1½-inch-deep dado cuts in the long leg pieces (A) to accommodate a 2x4 center rail (C). Cut rail to size and wait to install.
3 Double- or triple-bolt a 2x4 crosspiece (D) to the leg pieces to form each bench leg assembly (miter ends of the crosspiece to fit flush with slope of legs).
4 Join the two leg assemblies with the previously cut center rail (C). Screw or bolt into place.

5 Lay two slightly spaced 2x6 planks (E) on crosspieces (D) and screw into place to form bench seat.
6 To build the seat back/tabletop assembly, cut the two 2x8 end supports (F) into the tapered shape shown. Also cut a 2x4 crosspiece (G).
7 Screw three evenly spaced 2x6 planks (H) to the end supports (F) and crosspiece (G).
8 Attach seat back/tabletop to bench frame with one locking bolt on each end (see sketch).
9 Paint, stain, or treat unit with weathering oil.

10 If desired, make colorful, weatherproof cushions for your bench. See instructions for making cushions on page 95.

Materials (for one bench):

2×8 redwood or pine—4 ft.
   F 2 16 in.
2×6 redwood or pine—30 ft.
   E,H 5 72 in.
2×4 redwood or pine—18 ft.
   G 1 16 in.   **C** 1 60 in.
   A 2 31 in.   **B** 2 19 in.
   D 2 24 in.
Screws, nuts, bolts, washers, two locking bolts, and stain, paint, or weathering oil.

THE AMAZING CUBE

When you take a close look at most furniture construction, more often than not you'll find a cube-like box giving style, strength, and shape to the overall design. That's because the box is a truly versatile construction technique.

A Hang a door, install a shelf, and presto—you have a double-duty end table. Smooth mitered corners give a professional look.
B Here, a big, roomy drawer rolls out of its cubic shell. Like many box structures, this unit is built from a facing material (plywood) glued and nailed to a simple frame.
C Are boxes strong? You bet! Build a box and cushion the top for a great bench or stool. But remove the cushion and your box becomes a plant stand or night table.

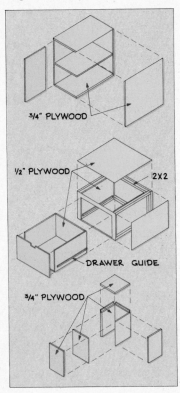

3/4" PLYWOOD

1/2" PLYWOOD   2X2

DRAWER GUIDE

3/4" PLYWOOD

FURNITURE BUILDING BASICS

Talk about creative outlets! Furniture building has to be one of the most interesting pastimes you can involve yourself with. It's demanding and exacting, but the results can truly be amazing.

Building furniture also has the added, pragmatic advantage of being a hobby that can save you a considerable amount of money. And most furniture pieces aren't at all difficult to construct, especially if you've read through the information that follows.

COMMON CONSTRUCTION MATERIALS

The materials you use for construction will vary, depending on the item's intended use. So when making your selection, ask yourself these questions: Are you constructing something for indoor or outdoor use? Is the item strictly utilitarian, or will it be suitable for use in a living room? Is it intended for light-duty use, or will it be a long-lived project subject to considerable use—and abuse?

Hardboard

Hardboard is available in 4x8-foot sheets and comes in ⅛- and ¼-inch thicknesses. Standard hardboard is an excellent choice for cabinetwork, drawer bottoms, and concealed panels.

You can also get hardboard perforated with holes spaced about one inch apart. Perforated hardboard is recommended for building storage for soiled laundry and for the backs of hi-fi cabinets. The quarter- and eighth-inch perforated hardboard lends itself to storing garden equipment and tools, too, as its holes accept hooks designed for this purpose. To expand or change the arrangement, just switch the hooks around. If the project will be subject to dampness, use tempered hardboard.

Particle board, chip board, and flake board, also members of the hardboard family, have a coarser grain structure, are lighter in color, and are available in thicknesses up to ¾ inch. These products are made of granulated or shredded wood particles forced together under pressure with a binder at high temperatures.

Plywood

Plywood also comes in 4x8-foot sheets, though larger sheets are available on special order. Thicknesses range from ⅛-inch to ¾-inch. For light-duty storage, the ¼- and ½-inch thicknesses are adequate. If you are planning to build an outdoor storage unit, specify *exterior grade* when making your purchase. Exterior grade plywood has its layers glued together with a waterproof glue to withstand rain.

The surfaces of plywood sheets are graded A, B, C, and D—with A the smoother, better surface and D the least desirable appearance. Choose AA (top grade, both sides) only for projects where both sides will be exposed; use a less expensive combination for others.

Solid Wood

Plain. ordinary wood still ranks as the most popular building material. Wood is sold by the "board foot" (1x12x12 inches). One board foot equals the surface area of one square foot, with a nominal thickness of one inch.

Wood is marketed by "grade." For most building projects No. 2 grade will satisfy your needs. This grade may have some blemishes, such as loose knots, but these don't reduce the strength of the wood.

If you're planning to build a unit that will be part of a room's decor, buy *select lumber*—a grade that's relatively free of blemishes.

Remember, too, that outdoor projects are a different subject. Redwood or cedar is preferable, but if you use a soft wood, be sure to treat it for moisture resistance.

Wood is divided into two categories. Softwoods come from trees that don't shed their leaves in the winter: hemlock, fir, pine, spruce, and similar evergreen cone-bearing trees. Hardwoods come from trees that do shed their leaves: maple, oak, birch, mahogany, walnut, and other broad-leaved varieties.

Wood is sold either as dimension lumber or millwork lumber, dimension being used for general construction, and millwork for some furniture building and other special uses.

Also keep in mind that lumber is sold by nominal size. A 2x4, for example, measures 1½x3½ inches. And a piece of ⁵⁄₄ material is less than 1¼ inches thick after milling.

The drawing shows nominal and actual sizes of most common pieces of dimension lumber. Ask lumberyard personnel for help with millwork lumber.

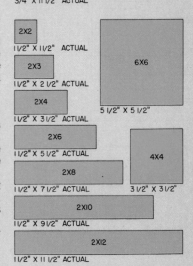

STANDARD LUMBER SIZES

IX2 — ¾" X 1½" ACTUAL
IX3 — ¾" X 2½" ACTUAL
IX4 — ¾" X 3½" ACTUAL
IX5 — ¾" X 4½" ACTUAL
IX6 — ¾" X 5½" ACTUAL
IX8 — ¾" X 7½" ACTUAL
IXI0 — ¾" X 9½" ACTUAL
IXI2 — ¾" X 11½" ACTUAL

4X6 — 3½" X 5½"
3X4 — 2½" X 3½"

2X2 — 1½" X 1½" ACTUAL
2X3 — 1½" X 2½" ACTUAL
2X4 — 1½" X 3½" ACTUAL
2X6 — 1½" X 5½" ACTUAL
2X8 — 1½" X 7½" ACTUAL
2XI0 — 1½" X 9½" ACTUAL
2XI2 — 1½" X 11½" ACTUAL

6X6 — 5½" X 5½"
4X4 — 3½" X 3½"

WOOD JOINERY TECHNIQUES

No matter what material you're planning to use, it will have to be cut to size—measure twice and cut once is a good rule—then put together using glue, nails or screws, and one of these joints.

Butt Joints

The simplest joint of all, the butt joint, consists of two pieces of wood meeting at a right angle and

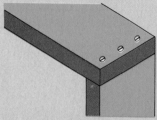

held together with nails, or preferably, screws (see sketch). A dab of glue before using the nails or screws will make the joint even more secure. But don't use glue if you're planning to take the work apart sometime later.

When reinforced by one of the six methods illustrated, the butt joint is effective for making corner

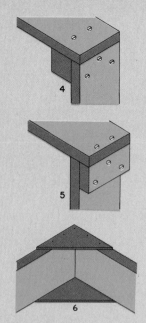

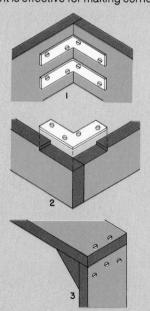

joints. Two common fasteners are corner braces (1), and flat corner plates (2). Using scrap wood, you can reinforce the joint with a triangular wedge (3), or with a square block (4). A variation of the square block places the block on the outside of the joint (5). Finally, a triangular gusset made from plywood or hardboard will also serve to reinforce a corner butt joint (6).

When a butt joint is in the form of a T—for example, in making a framework for light plywood or hardboard—you can reinforce it with a corner brace, T plate, or corrugated fasteners.

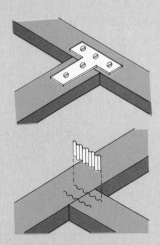

For really rough work, you can drive in a couple of nails at an angle, or toenail (see sketch). A variation of this is to place a block of wood alongside the crosspiece

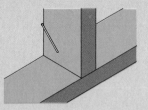

and secure it with a couple of nails.

A close cousin to the T joint and the butt joint is the plain overlap joint. It is held in place with at least two screws (see sketch). For extra reinforcement, apply glue between the pieces of wood.

Butt joints are an excellent means of securing backs to various units, especially when appearance is not a factor. Simply cut the back to the outside di-

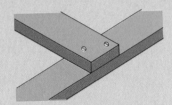

mensions of the work, then nail in place . . . it's called a flush back.

Lap Joints

On those projects where appearance is vital, consider full and half-lap joints. To make a full lap joint, cut a recess in one of the pieces of wood equal in depth to the thickness of the crossmember (see sketch).

The half-lap joint is similar to the full lap joint when finished, but the technique is different. First, cut a recess equal to half the

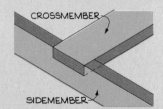

CROSSMEMBER

SIDEMEMBER

thickness of the crossmember halfway through the crossrail. Then, make a similar cut in the opposite half of the other piece (see sketch on the next page).

Butt joints and overlap joints do

not require any extra work besides cutting the pieces to size. However, full and half-lap joints

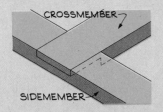

require the use of a backsaw and a chisel. For a full-lap joint, mark off the thickness and width of the crossmember on the work in which it is to fit.

Use the backsaw to make a cut at each end that's equal to the thickness of the crossmember, then use a chisel to remove the wood between the backsaw cuts. Check for sufficient depth and finish off with a fine rasp or sandpaper. Apply white glue to the mating surfaces and insert two screws to hold the joint securely.

Dado Joints

The dado joint is a simple way of suspending a shelf from its side supports. To make a dado joint, draw two parallel lines with a knife

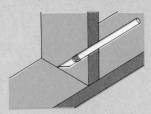

across the face of the work equal to the thickness of the wood it is to engage (see sketch). The depth should be about one-third of the thickness of the wood.

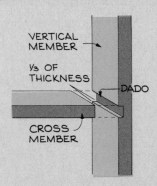

Next, make cuts on these lines and one or more between the lines

with a backsaw. Then, chisel out the wood to the correct depth.

You can speed the job immeasurably by using a router, a bench saw, or a radial arm saw. Any one of these power tools makes the cutting of dadoes an easy job — and provides much greater accuracy than can be achieved by hand.

If appearance is a factor, consider the stopped dado joint. In this type of joint, the dado (the cutaway part) extends only part way, and only a part of the shelf is cut away to match the non-cut part of the dado.

To make a stopped dado, first make your guide marks and chisel away a small area at the stopped end to allow for saw movement. Then make saw cuts

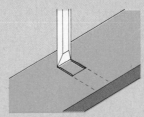

along your guide marks to the proper depth. Next chisel out the waste wood as shown in sketch.

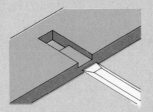

And finally, cut away a corner of the connecting board to accommodate the stopped dado.

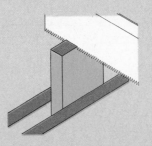

Rabbet Joints

The rabbet joint is really a partial dado. As you can see in the drawing at the top of the following column, only one of the meet-

ing members is cut away.

The rabbet joint is a simple one to construct, and it's quite strong, too. To ensure adequate strength, be sure to secure the meeting members with nails or screws and glue.

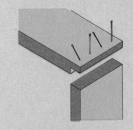

This joint is often used in the construction of inset backs for units such as cabinets and bookshelves (see the sketch below). To make this joint, rabbet each of the framing members, then care-

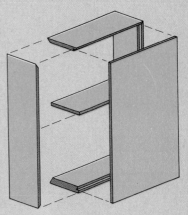

fully measure the distance between the rabbeted openings. Cut the back accordingly. Then use thin screws to secure the back to the unit.

Mortise and Tenon Joints

A particularly strong joint, the mortise and tenon joint is excellent when used for making T joints, right-angle joints, and for joints in the middle of rails. As its name indicates, this joint has two

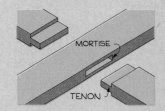

parts—the *mortise,* which is the open part of the joint, and the *tenon,* the part that fits into the mortise.

Make the mortise first, as it is much easier to fit the tenon to the mortise than the other way around. Divide the rail (the part to be mortised) into thirds and carefully mark off the depth and the width of the opening with a sharp pencil.

Next, use a chisel, equal to the width of the mortise, to remove the wood between the pencil marks. You can expedite this job by drilling a series of holes in the rail with an electric drill, a drill press, or even a hand drill. (If you have a drill press, you can purchase a special mortising bit that will drill square holes, believe it or not.) Mark the drill bit with a bit of tape to indicate the desired depth. Now use the chisel to remove the excess wood.

To make the tenon, divide the rail into thirds, mark the required depth, and use a backsaw to remove unwanted wood. If you have a bench or radial saw, the job of removing the wood will be much easier. Use a dado blade and set the blades high enough to remove the outer third of the wood. Reverse the work and remove the lower third, leaving the inner third intact.

To assemble, make a trial fit, and if all is well, apply some white glue to the tenon and insert it into the mortise. If by chance the tenon is too small for the mortise, simply insert hardwood wedges at top and bottom.

Use moderate clamping pressure on the joint until the glue dries overnight. Too much pressure will squeeze out the glue, actually weakening the joint.

Miter Joints

You can join two pieces of wood meeting at a right angle rather elegantly with a miter joint. And it's not a difficult joint to make. All you need is a miter box and a backsaw, or a power saw that you can adjust to cut at a 45 degree angle.

Since the simple miter joint is a surface joint with no shoulders for support, you must reinforce it. The easiest way to do this is with nails and glue (see sketch at the top of the following column). You'll notice that most picture

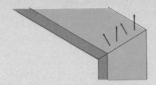

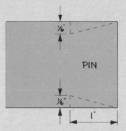

frames are made this way.

However, for cabinet and furniture work, you may use other means of reinforcement. One way is to use a hardwood spline as shown in the drawing. Apply glue to the spline and to the mitered

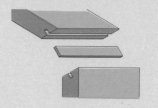

area and clamp as shown until the glue dries.

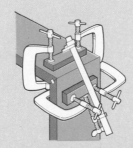

A variation of the long spline uses several short splines—at least three—inserted at opposing angles.

Dowels are a popular method of reinforcing a mitered joint, too. Careful drilling of the holes is necessary to make certain the dowel holes align. Use dowels that are slightly shorter than the holes they are to enter to allow for glue at the bottom. Score or roughen the

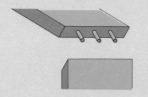

dowels to give the glue a better surface for a strong bond.

Dovetail Joints

The dovetail joint is a sign of good craftsmanship. It's a strong joint especially good for work subject

to heavy loads.

To make the joint, first draw the outline of the pin as shown and

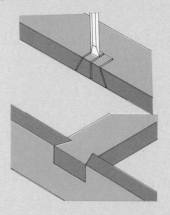

cut away the excess wood with a sharp backsaw. Place the pin over the second piece of wood and draw its outline with a sharp pencil. Make the two side cuts with the backsaw and an additional cut or two to facilitate the next step—chiseling away the excess wood. Then test for fit, apply glue and clamp the pieces until

dry. This is the basic way to make most dovetail joints. However, it's much easier to make dovetail joints with a router and dovetail template, especially made for home craftsman use.

Corner Joints

These joints are used for attaching legs to corners for framing. A good technique for joining corners is the three-way joint involving a set of steel braces you can buy. First, insert the bolt into the inside corner of the leg. Then cut slots into the side members, and secure the brace with two screws at each end. Finally, tighten the wing nut.

A variation of the three-way joint uses dowels and a triangular ¾-inch-thick gusset plate for additional reinforcement. To make this joint, first glue the dowels in

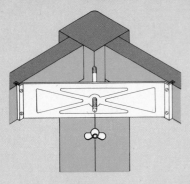

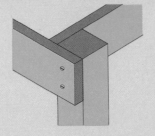

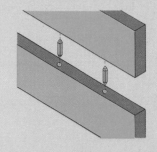

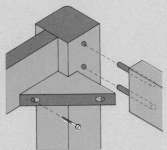

the vertical piece (see sketch). Let them dry completely, then finish the assembly.

A glued miter joint, reinforced with screws and glue, also makes a good corner joint. Make sure the screws do not penetrate the outside surface of the mitered joint.

Probably the strongest of the corner joints is the mortise and tenon (with mitered ends) reinforced with screws (see sketch). The miters on the ends of the tenons allow for a buildup of glue in the mortise, which in turn makes the joint stronger. Make sure that the holes you drill for the screws are not in line with each other.

of being fastened to each other, the butted members are each

fastened to the corner post with screws.

Edge-to-Edge Joints

Whenever an extra-wide surface is required, such as a desk top, workbench, or a large storage cabinet, this joint fills the bill. To make it, glue together two or more boards, then hold securely with either bar or pipe clamps. If the boards have a pronounced grain, reverse them side-to-side

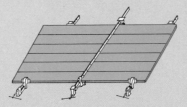

to minimize warping. For additional strength, screw cleats to the underside of the boards.

You also can use hardwood splines to join several boards. Cut a groove the exact width of the spline along the meeting sides of the two boards (see sketch). Cut the grooves slightly deeper than the spline width and in the exact center of the board thickness. The best way to cut such grooves is with a router or a bench saw.

make holes in the boards. You can either use a doweling jig or a drill. If you use a drill, first drive

brads (small finishing nails) into one board and press them against the second board to leave marks for drilling. Make the dowel holes slightly deeper than the dowels. Score the dowels, apply glue, join the two boards together, and clamp with pipe or bar clamps until the glue sets (allow plenty of time).

If you'll be drilling many dowel holes, you may want to use a wood or metal template to ensure accurate spacing.

Box Joints

One joint is so common in the construction of boxes — and drawers — it's called a *box joint*, or a *finger joint because its parts* look like the outstretched fingers of a hand (see sketch). Note that one of the mating pieces must have two end fingers, or one more

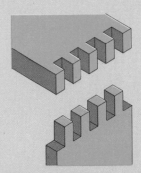

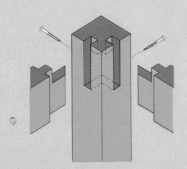

Otherwise, the wood may split. Use flathead screws and countersink the holes.

The simplest corner joint of all is a butt joint for the two horizontal members (see sketch). Instead

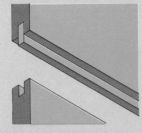

Then assemble with glue and clamps.

Another possibility for joining several boards involves the use of dowels. To make this joint, first

finger than the piece it is to engage. You can make this joint by hand with a backsaw and a small, sharp chisel. However, it is much easier, quicker, and more accurate to make it on a bench saw. Use a dado blade set to the desired width and proper depth of the fingers and mark off the waste area so there will be no mistake as to what you want to cut away.

THE HARDWARE YOU'LL NEED

For any sort of fastening work, you will need nails, screws, and bolts, as well as glues and cements.

Nails, Screws, and Bolts

These most common of all fastening materials are available in diverse widths and lengths, and in steel, brass, aluminum, copper, and even stainless steel.

Nails. Nails are sold by the penny—which has nothing to do with their cost. The "penny," (abbreviated *d*) refers to the size. The chart shows a box nail marked in the penny size designations as well as actual lengths in inches.

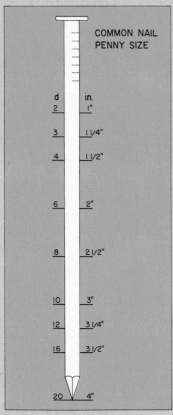

COMMON NAIL PENNY SIZE

d	in.
2	1"
3	1 1/4"
4	1 1/2"
6	2"
8	2 1/2"
10	3"
12	3 1/4"
16	3 1/2"
20	4"

Use common nails for general-purpose work; finish and casing nails for trim or cabinetwork; and brads for attaching molding to walls and furniture.

COMMON SCREWS

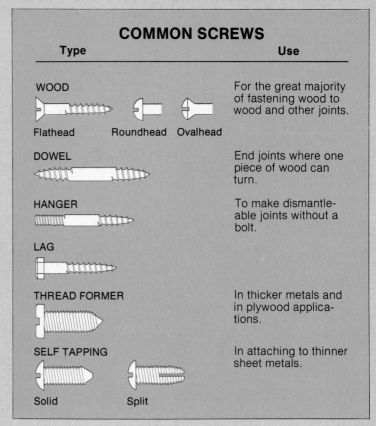

Type	Use
WOOD — Flathead, Roundhead, Ovalhead	For the great majority of fastening wood to wood and other joints.
DOWEL	End joints where one piece of wood can turn.
HANGER	To make dismantleable joints without a bolt.
LAG	
THREAD FORMER	In thicker metals and in plywood applications.
SELF TAPPING — Solid, Split	In attaching to thinner sheet metals.

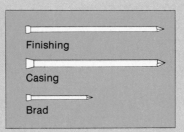

Finishing

Casing

Brad

Screws. Screws are sold by length and diameter. The diameter is indicated by a number, from 1 to 16. The thicker the screw shank, the larger the number. The drawing shows some of the most popular types of screws.

Always drill a pilot hole when inserting a screw into hardwood. And always drill a clearance hole in the leading piece of wood when screwing two pieces of wood together. Without a clearance hole, the leading piece tends to "hang up," preventing a tight fit between the two.

Bolts. You can also fasten wood together with bolts, but only if there is access to the back for the required washer and nut. A bolted joint is stronger than a screwed joint, as the bolt diameter is generally thicker than the comparable screw, and also because the wrench used to tighten the nut can apply much more force than a screwdriver in a screw slot.

Glues and Cements

While not "hardware" as such, glue is an important adjunct to any fastening job. The so-called white glue is excellent for use with wood, and only moderate clamping pressure is required. When dry, it is crystal clear. However, it's not waterproof so don't use it for work subject to excessive dampness—and of course, never for outdoor use. Use the two-tube epoxy "glue" for joints that must be waterproof.

Plastic resin glue, a powder that you mix with water to a creamy consistency, is highly water resistant.

Contact cement provides an excellent bond between wood and wood, and wood and plastic. When working with contact cement, remember that it dries instantly and position your surfaces

COMMON BOLTS

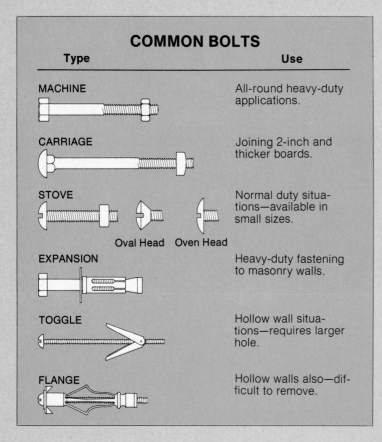

Type	Use
MACHINE	All-round heavy-duty applications.
CARRIAGE	Joining 2-inch and thicker boards.
STOVE — Oval Head / Oven Head	Normal duty situations—available in small sizes.
EXPANSION	Heavy-duty fastening to masonry walls.
TOGGLE	Hollow wall situations—requires larger hole.
FLANGE	Hollow walls also—difficult to remove.

The plate type caster is merely screwed to the bottom by four screws that pass through holes in the plate. They are not height adjustable unless, of course, you use shims.

All casters use ball bearings as part of the plate assembly to facilitate swiveling. For extra-heavy usages, purchase casters with ball-bearing wheels as well.

The wheels on casters are of two types—plastic or rubber. Use casters with plastic wheels if the project is to be rolled on a soft surface such as a rug; rubber wheeled casters are best on hard concrete, vinyl, or hardwood. It's a good idea to use graphite to lubricate the wheels and their bearings, as oil tends to pick up dust and dirt.

To prevent a caster-equipped unit from rolling, get locking casters. A small lever on the outside of the wheel locks a "brake." Brakes on only two of the four casters on a unit are sufficient.

Miscellaneous Hardware

There are many types of hardware that can come in handy when you're constructing storage bins, cabinets, chests, shelves, and other projects.

Following are some you may need from time to time: corrugated fasteners connect two boards or mend splits in wood; angle irons reinforce corners; flat and T plates also reinforce work; masonry nails secure work to concrete or brick walls; steel plates with a threaded center are used for attaching legs to cabinets; screw eyes and cup hooks allow for hanging items inside storage units; and lag screw plugs made of lead or plastic secure furring strips or shelf brackets to masonry walls.

You'll be wise to stock your workshop with most of these items in a couple of sizes. That way, you won't have to make a special trip when they're needed.

When to Use What Glue

Type	Use
White glue (No mixing)	Paper, cloth, wood
Epoxy (requires mixing)	Wood, metal, stone (waterproof)
Plastic resin (requires mixing)	Wood to wood (water resistant)
Contact cement (no mixing)	Wood to wood or plastic (waterproof)
Waterproof glue (requires mixing)	Wood to wood (waterproof)

together exactly as you want them. You won't get a second chance.

True waterproof glue comes in two containers; one holds a liquid resin, the other a powder catalyst. When dry, this glue is absolutely waterproof and can be safely used for garden equipment and all outdoor projects and furniture.

Glides and Casters

The intended use determines whether a piece of furniture needs a caster or a glide. If you don't plan to move it frequently, use a glide; otherwise, a caster is the best choice.

Glides come in many sizes, determined by the glide area touching the floor, and with steel or plastic bottoms. The simple nail-on glides aren't height adjustable but you can adjust screw glides by screwing the glide in or out to prevent wobbling if the floor is uneven, or if by some chance, the project does not have an even base.

Casters are made in two styles—stem type (only the stem type is adjustable) and plate type (at left in sketch). The stem type requires a hole to be drilled into the leg or base of the cabinet or furniture. This hole accepts a sleeve that in turn accepts the stem of the caster.

HOW TO MAKE DRAWERS

Next to shelves, drawers are the most convenient place for storage. And a drawer is comparatively easy to build. It's just a five-sided box, connected at its corners with the joints previously described.

Types of Drawers

Drawers, no matter how they're made, fall into two general classifications—the flush or recessed type, and the lip type.

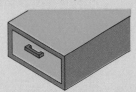

Flush drawers. You must fit this type of drawer carefully to the cabinet opening, with only enough clearance at top and sides to facilitate sliding in and out. In fact, some custom cabinetmakers often will make flush-type drawers with a taper of 1/16 inch from front to back to ensure a good appearance and an easy-sliding fit.

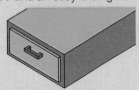

Lipped drawers. These drawers have an oversize front panel that completely covers the drawer opening and so offers much greater leeway in fitting the drawer into its recess.

One way to make a lipped drawer is to rabbet the front panel to the sides and bottom of the drawer, leaving an overlap of ½ inch or so. A simpler way is to screw a false front to the finished drawer front. With this method, if there is any error in construction, the false front will hide it. Attach the drawer front with countersunk flathead screws from the *inside* of the drawer. In addition to the screws, apply white glue between the two pieces.

Construction Details

When making drawers, remember to make the cabinet first, then fit the drawers to the cabinet openings. To make a drawer, first determine its length and cut two pieces of wood to this size and the required width. (The width, of course, will be the height of the finished drawer.)

Draw two parallel lines, equal to the thickness of the drawer back, about ½ inch from the ends

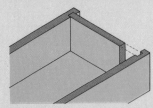

of the two pieces. Cut a dado between these lines to a depth of ¼ inch.

Next, measure the inside distance between the two sides of the drawer opening and cut the drawer back to this measurement. (Allow for clearance and the depth of the dado cuts in the drawer sides.)

For the front of the drawer, plan simple butt joints and cut it to allow a ¼-inch overhang on all sides, if you plan a lip.

You are now ready to partially assemble the drawer. Brush some white glue into the two dado cuts and install the back panel. Use three or four brads at each joint to secure the sides. Next attach the drawer front using glue and brads or screws to secure it to the sides.

A false front nailed or screwed to the existing front from the inside of the drawer will conceal the original brads or screws. If you use brads, countersink them with a nail set.

The bottom of the drawer consists of ¼-inch or thicker plywood, and is nailed to the sides and back of the drawer. For stronger, more elaborate construction, you can use any one of the woodworking joints described earlier in this section.

Drawer Runners and Guides

To ensure that the drawers you build will move in and out without wobbling, you can use any one of

three methods: guides located at each side of the drawer; a central guide placed at the bottom of the drawer; or commercial metal tracks mounted on the sides of the cabinet with nylon wheels on the drawer sides. These come in lengths to fit most drawers and are especially good for heavy loads. Select them before you build the drawer in order to plan the clearance space.

The simplest guide consists of two narrow lengths of wood secured to each side of the drawer, spaced an inch apart (see sketch). Another strip of wood, mounted on each side of the

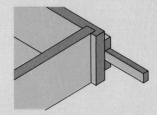

drawer opening, fits the "track" mounted on the drawer sides. To ease operation, apply paste wax to all touching surfaces.

For guides at the bottom of the drawer, mount lengths of wood on the cabinet and engage the two strips of wood on the bottom of the drawer.

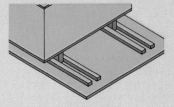

If you're planning to incorporate runners and guides in the drawers, make allowances before starting work. A clearance of ½-inch is required for guides mounted at the sides of the drawers, and 1 inch for center-mounted guides. Regardless of what type of drawer guides you use, make sure you install them accurately.

You can even make easy-sliding drawers without guides or runners by installing plastic glides in the drawer openings so the bottom of the drawer will bear against plastic instead of wood. Steel thumbtacks also ease drawer movement. But don't forget to apply wax to the bottom bearing surfaces of the drawer.

HOW TO INSTALL CABINET DOORS

Except for shelves, tables, and chairs, nearly every piece of furniture you build will have some sort of door. All doors require hinges or tracks, and handles for opening and closing. Here are the basics.

Construction Pointers

To prevent warping, cabinet doors should be at least ½ inch thick. However, you can use a ¼-inch panel, providing you frame it with ½-inch wood, somewhat like a picture frame.

If you plan to laminate a door panel with plastic, use the thin grade laminate especially made for vertical surfaces. The heavy grade, made for countertops, may cause the cabinet to warp.

Sliding Doors

Sliding doors are easier to fit and install than swinging doors, and, as a rule, are of much lighter stock than conventional doors. Track for sliding doors can be aluminum or plastic (left sketch), or it can consist of grooves cut into the top and bottom of the framework (right sketch).

Of course, you must cut these grooves before assembly. Make the upper grooves about twice as deep as the bottom ones so you can lift up, then lower the door into place. The doors should be flush with the bottom shelf surface when it's touching the top of the upper groove.

To ease sliding, apply wax or a silicone spray to the grooves. If you're planning to use handles, recess them into the door so there will be no interference when the doors bypass each other.

Hinged Doors

Flush-type hinged doors that recess within the framing require clearance all around to prevent binding. To install a flush-type door, make a dry fit, and if the door fits, insert small wedges at all sides to hold it in place and ensure clearance until the hinges have been completely installed.

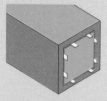

Then place the hinge against the door—if it's an exterior mounting—and mark the hinge holes with an awl. Drill pilot holes and install the hinges. Use this same procedure if you have an interior mounting job.

With hinges that are partly concealed—half on the inside of the door and half on the frame—mount the hinges on the door first, set the door in place, and mark the location of the hinge on the frame or door jamb. This method is much easier than trying to fit an already-mounted hinge to the blind or interior part of the door.

Types of hinges. There are literally dozens of types of hinges to choose from. Following are a few of the more common varieties.

As a general rule, you should mortise hinges into cabinets so they are flush with the work. However, always surface mount decorative hinges, such as colonial, rustic, and ornamental hinges.

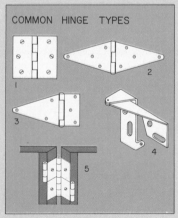

(1) *Butt hinges* are the type you're probably most familiar with. Use them for either right- or left-hand doors. The larger sizes have re-

movable pins to facilitate taking off the door; the smaller sizes don't. For long cabinet doors or lids. use a piano hinge (a long butt hinge) rather than several smaller ones. (2, 3) The *strap hinge* and the *T hinge* are used for extra-heavy doors. There's no need to mortise these hinges, as they are strictly functional.

(4) *Pivot hinges,* also called knife hinges, are available in different shapes and are especially good for use on ¾-inch plywood doors. All shapes present a very unobtrusive appearance.

(5) *Double-acting hinges* allow a door to be swung from either direction.

Self-closing hinges operate by means of a spring concealed within the barrel of the hinge. Another type, used on kitchen cabinets, has no spring, yet closes the door with a positive snapping action. Its secret is a square shoulder next to the pin.

Special-purpose hinges are available with offset leaves (so the door will overlap the framing); hinges with knuckles (for quick door removal); ball-bearing hinges lubricated for life (for extra-heavy doors); hinges that will automatically raise a door when it is opened (so that it will clear a carpet on the far side of the door); burglar-resistant hinges (with pins that can't be removed when they're on the outside); and hinges that allow a door to be swung back far enough so that the full width of the doorway can be utilized.

Door catches and handles. In addition to hinges, you will need hardware to keep the doors closed and to lock them. For cabinet work, your best hardware bets are spring-loaded or magnetic catches.

Spring-loaded catches come with single and double rollers and are ideal for lipped doors, flush doors, double doors, and shelves. These catches are adjustable.

Install magnetic catches so there is physical contact between the magnet in the frame and the "keeper" on the door.

A handle of some type is required for all drawers and doors. Handles can be surface-mounted or recessed flush with the drawer or door. Sliding doors always use recessed handles so the doors can bypass each other.

FINISHING TECHNIQUES

Finishing is your final job before you can step back and admire your work. Before starting, make sure that all nails are flush or countersunk and filled, all flathead screws are flush with the surface, all cracks are filled, and all surfaces are sanded and cleaned.

Hardboard and Chip Board

If the unit you have built is made of hardboard, about the only finish you can apply to it is paint. No preparation is needed except to remove any oil or dirt. Inasmuch as hardboard is brown—the tempered type is a darker brown—you'll need to apply at least two coats of paint if you want the final finish to be a light color.

Hardboard will accept latex or alkyd paints equally well. Between coats, let dry overnight and then sand lightly.

You also can paint chip board, flake board, and particle board, but because of their slightly rougher texture you should apply a "filler" coat of shellac first, then proceed with painting.

Plywood

Because of its comparatively low cost, fir plywood is used extensively for building projects. However, the hard and soft growth patterns in the wood will show through unless a sealer is used before painting or finishing with varnish or lacquer.

After sealing, sand lightly and finish with at least two coats of paint, varnish, or lacquer. The final step for varnish or lacquer work consists of an application of paste wax applied with fine steel wool and polishing with terry cloth or any other coarse-textured cloth.

Plywood has a pronounced end grain due to its layered construction. If your project will be on display, it's best to hide the end grain, and there are several ways to do this.

A mitered joint is the obvious solution, as then the end grain is hidden within the joint. Another solution is wood veneer tape (see sketch). This tape comes in rolls and is really walnut, oak, mahogany, or a similar wood in a very thin strip about ¾ inch wide. Either glue it or use contact cement, applying the cement to the tape and to the plywood edges. When the cement has lost its gloss, carefully align the tape and press over the plywood edge.

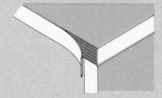

You also can use molding to cover the edges. It has the additional advantage of making a decorative edge requiring no further treatment.

Metal molding is another option, especially useful for edges which are subject to wear and abuse.

A rabbet joint will also hide end grain. Make the rabbet deep enough so that only the last ply is uncut.

Other Woods

If your project is constructed of a fine wood, a more elaborate finishing technique is needed.

Sanding. You can do this by hand or with a power sander. A power belt sander is fine for initial sanding, but always do the final sanding with an orbital or straight line finishing sander—or with fine sandpaper.

Filling and staining. Open grain woods such as oak, chestnut, walnut, ash, and mahogany require a filler to close their pores. Apply the filler with a brush or rag, wiping across the grain. After 10 or 15 minutes, remove the excess filler with a coarse cloth.

If a stain is called for, let the wood dry for 24 hours before application. A stain applied over a filler that has not dried will show up as a "hot" spot.

Sealing. A sealer, as its name implies, is used to seal the stains and filler from the subsequent finishing coats.

One of the best sealers is shellac. One advantage of using shellac is that it prevents the stain from bleeding. Thin the shellac with alcohol to the consistency of light cream; as it comes in the can, it's much too thick for use as a sealer. You can also use ready-mixed stains combined with a sealer.

Finishes. *Varnish,* the traditional finish for wood, is available in many types and colors.

To prepare a piece for varnish, sand it lightly, wipe off the dust with a turpentine-dampened rag, and apply the varnish with long, flowing strokes. Do not brush out the varnish as you would paint. And don't use varnish during humid weather. To make sure the varnish will flow evenly, place the can in warm water.

Varnish requires at least two coats, with a minimum of 24 hours drying time. Sand lightly between coats. After the second or third coat has dried for at least a week, rub down with steel wool and paste wax. Polish with a rough cloth.

Shellac, too, will yield super results. It's fairly easy to work with and it dries dust free in a half-hour. You can apply the second coat within two hours. Sanding is not required between coats, as the second coat tends to partially dissolve and melt into the first one.

One disadvantage of shellac is that it shows a ring if a liquor-stained glass is placed on a shellac-finished surface. Also, shellac sometimes tends to crack if exposed to dampness.

Polyurethane is a tough synthetic varnish that resists abrasion, alcohol, and fruit stains. It's great for floors, furniture, walls, and woodwork. To apply polyurethane the surface must be clean, dry, and free of grease, oil, and wax. Don't apply a polyurethane finish over previously shellacked or lacquered surfaces. Allow at least 12 hours drying time for each coat, and clean your brushes with mineral spirits or turpentine.

Lacquer is a fast-drying finish you can apply by spray or brush. For spraying, thin lacquer only with lacquer thinner. *Never use turpentine or mineral spirits.*

To brush lacquer, always use a brush that has *never* been used to apply paint.

And never apply lacquer over a painted surface, as the lacquer will lift the paint. As with shellac, sanding between coats is not necessary.

HOW TO UPHOLSTER CUSHIONS

By now, you've probably stepped back to admire your new furniture project. But if you have any doubts about its comfort, here's your chance to make your project as cozy as it is attractive.

Pieced Cushion Covers

For a pieced cushion cover, you'll need a top, bottom, and a strip for the sides (called the boxing strip). For a square or rectangular cushion, begin by measuring the width and length of the top and bottom (see the sketch below). For a round cushion, measure the diameter and draw a circle to size to serve as a pattern.

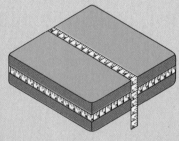

To determine the size of the boxing strip, measure the thickness of the cushion and its outside perimeter, then cut the fabric to these measurements. Don't add seam allowances. As you stitch the cover, use ½-inch seam allowances to make the cover 1 inch smaller than your cushion. This ensures a snug, neat fit.

For a cushion with a zipper, cut a length of boxing strip 1 inch longer than the zipper. Cut this piece lengthwise through center. With the right sides of the fabric facing, machine-baste one long edge together in a 1-inch seam. Press the seam open and insert the zipper.

To determine the length of the remainder of the boxing strip, subtract the length of the zipper from the total length of the boxing strip. Add 1 inch to this measurement. Using ½-inch seam

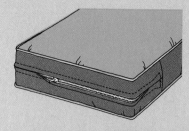

allowance, join the ends of this boxing strip to the zipper section (see sketch). Open the zipper. Stitch the boxing strip to the top and bottom pieces. Trim seams. Turn the cover right side out, press, and insert cushion.

To cover a round bolster, cut fabric circles for the end pieces the same size as the diameter of the bolster. Measure the length and circumference of bolster. Cut a fabric rectangle this size. Stitch the circles to the rectangle. To make a removable cover, you'll need to insert a zippered strip in part of rectangle.

One-Piece Covers

This technique requires less time and fabric than making a pieced cover. To determine the amount of fabric needed, wrap the tape snugly around form to determine width (A) and height (B). Measure the depth (C) as shown. Use the full amount of measurement B, plus a 1-inch seam allowance for the length of the rectangle, and ½ of measurement A, plus a 1-inch seam allowance, for the width of the rectangle.

Mark off a rectangle of this size on wrong side of fabric. Cut out the piece. You'll need a zipper that is 2 inches shorter than cushion's width.

To assemble the cover, fold the rectangle, right sides together, in half crosswise. If your cover has a zipper, center the zipper on the ½-inch end seam and mark the zipper opening. Using ½-inch seam allowances, stitch to these points from the

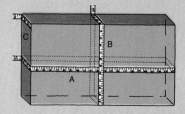

edges and reinforce with backstitching. Machine-baste the opening and press open.

Center the zipper over the basted seam and baste. Turn the cover to the right side and stitch the zipper in place. Remove the basting and open the zipper. Turn cover to the wrong side again, and stitch the side seams with ½-inch seam allowances.

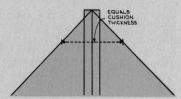

To shape each corner, fold one corner with the side seam centered, as shown. Across the point, draw a line that equals the depth of the cushion form (measurement C). Cut off the corner ½ inch above this line and stitch on the line; backstitch to reinforce.

Cushion Forms

Ready-made forms are available in a variety of shapes and sizes. Box-edge cushions, which can be square, rectangular, or round, give the best results for most furniture projects.

Most box-edge forms are slabs of polyurethane foam available in several thicknesses. You can cut these easily to fit your project by using a razor blade and a straightedge. And, for a softer cushion, stack two or more thicknesses of thinner foam together.

Bolster forms usually are molded and come in various sizes, lengths, and shapes (triangular, tubular, wedge, or five-sided).

However, you can construct almost any shape cushion if you make your own form. First decide on the size. Use muslin as the cover material, following directions given above for upholstering cushions. Assemble and stuff muslin forms.

For filling, use shredded foam, polyester fiber fill, or kapok. Or use cotton batting that's sold in a roll about 16 inches wide and 1 inch thick. You can cut and stack it, or roll it to fit your dimensions. (Cotton batting is also good for use as a filler to adjust foam forms to a particular size).

COMMON FURNITURE DIMENSIONS

How tall should you build a desk? How much room do you need for a standard-size double bed? How wide should your new kitchen table be? When you're creating your own furniture designs, it's important to know exactly what dimensions are comfortable for most people. Use the ones given here as a guide to the size of most common furniture pieces.

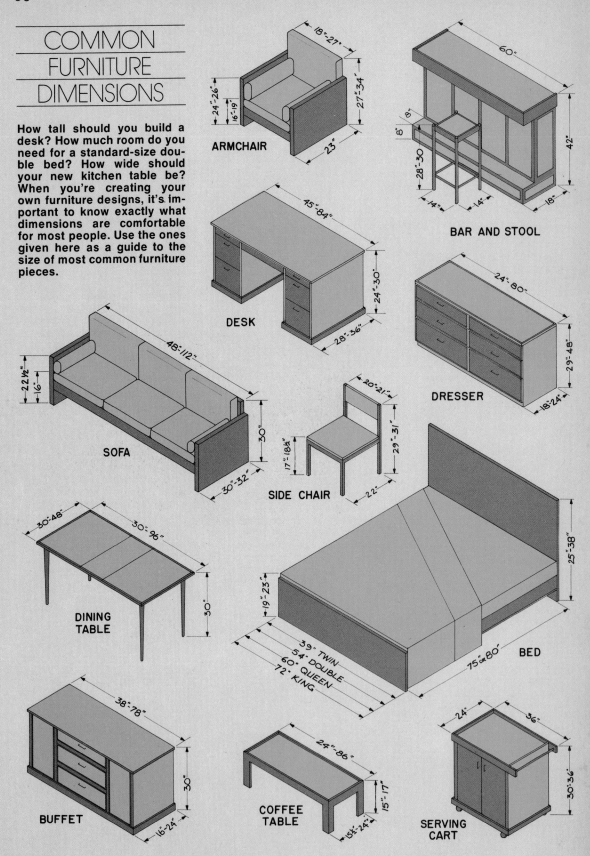

ARMCHAIR

BAR AND STOOL

DESK

SOFA

SIDE CHAIR

DRESSER

DINING TABLE

BED

BUFFET

COFFEE TABLE

SERVING CART